ESPRESSO
for the
SPIRIT

ESPRESSO
for the
SPIRIT

THIRDSERVING

Daily Reflections from God's Word to Get You Growing

DALE A. O'SHIELDS

PRACTICAL
LIVING
PRESS

Gaithersburg, Maryland

Published in Gaithersburg, Maryland, by Practical Living Press
ISBN 978-0-9898891-3-1
Learn more about the author at www.DaleOShields.com

DEDICATION

To all who seek for greater strength

and wisdom

in their relationship

with Jesus Christ.

CONTENTS

INTRODUCTION

One of the most important things we can do as Christian believers is take time each day to read and reflect on God's Word. As we do, our goal needs to be life change. God is not interested in filling our heads with a lot of biblical information. He is very interested in transforming our hearts. His Word, when studied with the aid of the Holy Spirit, is designed for our edification and application. His Word has the power to change us, as we determine to live out what we are learning.

These daily devotional readings will help you in this process. As you prayerfully reflect on the Scriptures and thoughts presented, you will be challenged to take actions that will make each message a part of your life.

Each reading contains a "Get Growing" challenge and a place for you to record your personal reflections. My prayer is that each of these devotionals will draw you closer to Jesus Christ, help you discover the potential God placed in you, and equip you to be a more joyous and productive servant in the kingdom of God.

Let's grow!

Pastor Dale

The vigor [strength] of our spiritual lives

will be in exact proportion

to the place held by the Bible

in our lives and thoughts.

~ George Mueller

Attitude Management

A relaxed attitude lengthens a man's life.
Proverbs 14:30 (TLB)

You must have the same attitude that Christ Jesus had.
Philippians 2:5 (NLT)

When was the last time you encountered someone with an attitude? We instinctively sense when a person has "attitude" and generally think of attitudes in negative terms. But attitudes can also be positive. In fact, "having an attitude" can be good, if we have the right one.

These two Scriptures give us guidance about managing our attitudes. Proverbs reminds us of the benefits of a right attitude, which means a "relaxed attitude." The original biblical word for "relaxed" refers to a *"composed, peaceful, and tranquil"* attitude. This gives us valuable insight.

Attitudes start in the heart. If our heart is composed, peaceful, and tranquil, then our words, interactions, and behaviors will demonstrate the same. If we are disturbed on the inside, we will create disturbances in the relationships and environments around us. When we manage our attitudes well, we add length and quality to our lives, and to the lives of others.

In Philippians, Paul teaches us that attitudes are chosen *by* us, not imposed *on* us. Through the help of the Holy Spirit, we can develop the same attitudes Jesus possessed. Jesus consistently demonstrated attitudes of faith, submission, selflessness, and humility. Even during his toughest times, Jesus kept his heart and mind composed, peaceful, and tranquil.

When Jesus' attitudes were threatened, he retreated to the presence of his Heavenly Father for strength and power. The classic example of this is Jesus' prayer in the Garden of

Gethsemane. Before he went to the Cross, Jesus made sure that his heart and head—his attitudes—were where they were supposed to be.

Just like Jesus, our attitudes are tested. Negative thoughts and influences work their way into our hearts and minds, and erode our spiritual and emotional composure. Our attitudes "go south," affecting us, and the people around us.

Good attitudes are especially hard to maintain in tough times. When circumstances seem to conspire against us, when people do not treat us right, when there is "more month than money," when we are weary of waiting for something, when we have little time to rest—these things challenge our attitudes.

For times like these, here are some practical suggestions that help us keep our attitudes where they need to be:

- Keep regular appointments with your Heavenly Father.
- Stay connected to people who consistently manage their attitudes well and inspire you to do the same.
- Avoid people who have a negative influence on your thinking.
- Schedule time for rest and recreation.
- Count your blessings.
- Trust in God's love for you.
- Remember, recite, and believe the promises of God's Word.

Get Growing!

What bad attitudes have been a pattern in your life? It has been said that our *attitudes* affect our *altitude* in life. With God's help, grab hold of your attitudes and soar to a new level of living!

Healing the Heart

The Lord does not look at the things people look at.
People look at the outward appearance, but the Lord
looks at the heart. 1 Samuel 16:7 (NIV)

When the prophet Samuel was called by God to appoint a new king over Israel, following the spiritual decline of King Saul, God sent him to the home of a man named Jesse. One of Jesse's sons would be anointed with oil as Israel's next king.

Jesse sent his first son, Eliab, to be interviewed by Samuel. The prophet's initial impression was "this must be the one." Eliab had the physical stature and mannerisms of a head of state. God spoke some words to Samuel in that moment that teach us a very important truth about God and his view of us. After telling Samuel that he had someone else in mind for Israel's kingship, God said to Samuel that he looks at the heart.

The Lord reminded Samuel, and us, that he sees deep inside of us. He knows things about us that no one else knows, including the condition of our hearts.

While we often think of this in the negative sense—that God knows the hidden sins of our hearts—it is also important for us to consider another aspect of God's statement to Samuel. God not only knows the sinful condition of our hearts, he also knows the hurts, pains, and wounds we are carrying in our hearts. He knows and he cares about the inner brokenness that weighs us down, restricts our relationships, and hinders our effectiveness for the kingdom of God.

In addition to knowing and caring, God is committed to healing our hearts. Look at the words of the psalmist that describe God's attitude and actions toward people experiencing inner pain: *"He heals the brokenhearted and binds up their wounds" (Psalm 147:3 NIV).*

If you are carrying around pain, scars of the heart, deep wounds that have plagued your progress, know that God wants to make you whole. He is willing to take your pain and release his healing grace into the deepest part of your soul. He is our "heart healer."

Get Growing!

- What are the things God can see in your heart that nobody else can see?
- Read 1 Samuel 16. What is the Lord telling you about the condition of your heart?

Too Soon to Quit

So Naaman went down to the Jordan River and dipped himself seven times, as the man of God had instructed him. And his skin became as healthy as the skin of a young child, and he was healed! 2 Kings 5:14 (NLT)

You have heard it before—"Winners never quit and quitters never win!" The famous American football coach Vince Lombardi frequently reminded his players of this life principle: you will not win if you quit too soon.

There are many victories, breakthroughs, successes and achievements that only come after long seasons of what seems like fruitless effort. Tedious research, tireless practice, persistent efforts, patient investment, persevering prayer, long-term labor usually pays off—eventually.

The reality is that many of these pay-offs never come—simply because people give up. They quit too soon. Days, weeks, years, decades of working and waiting, with little to show for it, can take its toll on your heart and soul. Let's be honest, it's hard to keep going when everything inside you is screaming, "Quit!"

While there are times to throw in the towel in pursuit of something, there are many more times when we need to remain in the ring. Many people leave and lose when victory is right around the corner.

There's a great story in the Bible that reminds us of the power of persistence, especially in our obedience to God. It's the Old Testament story of Naaman (2 Kings 5).

Naaman contracted the deadly disease of leprosy. He was directed to the prophet Elisha for a miracle cure. Elisha gave Naaman instructions that he did not like. These instructions confronted Naaman's pride and tested his patience. He was told to go and dip himself seven times in the muddy Jordan River. God promised that in doing this he would be healed. After much protest, Naaman finally agreed to obey God's instructions.

It is very important to see that Naaman's healing happened *after* the seventh dip. Dips one through six seemed to make no difference in his condition. Nothing improved and nothing changed until Naaman completed his seventh immersion in the muddy waters of the Jordan. But his persistent obedience paid off. On the seventh dip, healing came, breakthrough happen, the victory was won.

What if Naaman had stopped on dip two, or four, or five, or six? His story wouldn't be in the Bible. We know about this man *only* because he didn't quit too soon!

Get Growing!

What about you? What are you about to quit? A job? A marriage? An exercise program? A commitment? A prayer? A _____? Think hard before you do. Maybe it's too soon to quit!

Favor and Wisdom

And God gave him favor before Pharaoh, king of Egypt. God also gave Joseph unusual wisdom, so that Pharaoh appointed him governor over all of Egypt and put him in charge of the palace. Acts 7:10 (NLT)

God has a unique plan and purpose for your life. There's a work he wants you to do that no one can do quite the way you can. Certain resources are essential for effectiveness and success in God's assignments for your life. Two of these essentials are favor and wisdom.

In the Old Testament, we find the story of a young man named Joseph. God had a plan and purpose for his life. God wanted to use Joseph to lead a nation through a time of trouble. He wanted to use Joseph to establish a safe haven for his family in the midst of terrible famine.

The story of Joseph's life is fascinating and very instructive. A dream that called Joseph to his life purpose at 17 years of age was fulfilled many years later. Over those long years, God took this young man through all kinds of situations to break him, mold him, and transform his character. Joseph needed to develop the inner qualities that would make him ready to handle the responsibilities God assigned him.

After years of walking through refining circumstances designed by God to mature him, Joseph was prepared for his biggest God-given life assignment. He was ready to be used by God as a leader. Joseph was no longer driven by a dream; he was deeply dependent on his Lord.

The Bible is very specific about the qualities—the resources—that enabled Joseph to be effective and successful in his God-given assignment. Note the two things God gave Joseph that gave him success: FAVOR and WISDOM.

Favor is the Greek word "*charis*." It's the root word for the English term "*charisma*." Favor is the gracious gift of influence, open doors, acceptance, prepared and paved pathways for building meaningful, strategic relationships and experiencing unprecedented positive opportunities. It comes from God and releases blessings to us that we could never accomplish or achieve by ourselves. When we see it and experience it, all we can do is appreciate it, and praise and give God the glory for it.

Wisdom is deep insight, understanding, prudence, and incisive perception. It's the right application of knowledge. This, too, is a gift from God. While we're told to work hard in gaining wisdom, it ultimately comes from God, who is the source of all wisdom.

Joseph couldn't get his job done without God's favor and wisdom. Neither can we.

Get Growing!

- Think about a time in your life you witnessed God's favor. What did you learn about that situation?
- Have you asked God to grant you wisdom to handle his assignments for your life?
- How can you use the gifts God has given you to effectively and successfully accomplish life assignments?

Unhappy?

Give me happiness, O Lord, for I give myself to you.
Psalm 86:4 (NLT)

"I'm not happy with_____." "I'm not happy about
_____." It's likely that something readily comes to your
mind to complete those sentences. Perhaps it is *"the weather,
my job, my marriage, my boss, my children,"* or even, *"my
looks."*

Life offers many reasons to be unhappy. We're usually
quick to grab things that drag down our thoughts and feelings.
Research shows that up to 70% of Americans are unhappy at
any given time. So, seven out of every ten people you encounter
today are somewhat miserable. Unhappiness is an epidemic!

What can be done? There really isn't anything you can do for
or give to someone else to cure their unhappiness. Happiness is
a personal issue. But here are ten things you can do for yourself
that are guaranteed to help you become happier:

1. Take time for God. Think about the good things
   God has done for you. Make a list of blessings, of
   God's gifts and care for you, and tell God "thank you."
2. Work on your face. Work on your countenance, not
   just your make-up or hair. Is your countenance
   characterized by frowns or smiles? Consciously smile
   more and your heart will reflect your face.
3. Surprise strangers with words and acts of
   generosity, kindness, and service. Do something
   today for someone you don't know to bless and
   brighten their day.
4. Surprise someone you know with words and acts of
   generosity, kindness, and service. Sometimes we're

apt to do nice things for people we don't know more than for the people closest to us.

5. Let others go first. Whether it's in traffic, at an elevator, at a door, at the grocery store, slow down and let others go first.

6. Connect with someone who's hurting. Move past yourself and communicate care to someone who's hurting. Call, write, send flowers, pray. Be a burden-bearer.

7. Say "please" and "thank you." These phrases really do make a difference to others, and they make you happier, too.

8. Overlook offenses. Make today a "grace day." When someone says or does something that would normally hurt your feelings, aggravate anger, or generate a nasty reaction, choose to forgive and overlook it. Let people who offend you go free. Be a forgiver today.

9. Tell people in your life why you love and appreciate them. Tell them why you love them and what you love about them.

10. Decide that you're only going to say good things about people. Choose to have a gossip-free, grumble-free, nitpick-free day. If you can't say something good about someone, don't say anything at all!

Get Growing!

Set goals. Put in practice at least one thing from each point above each day.

Prepared?

But mark this: there will be terrible times in the last days. People will be lovers of themselves, lovers of money, boastful, proud, abusive, disobedient to their parents, ungrateful, unholy, without love, unforgiving, slanderous, without self-control, brutal, not lovers of the good, treacherous, rash, conceited, lovers of pleasure rather than lovers of God—having a form of godliness but denying its power. Have nothing to do with such people.
2 Timothy 3:1-5 (NIV)

Could we be on the brink of the end of history? What does the future hold for us? As we observe events transpiring in our world, it causes us to think about these questions.

Many individuals through the years have predicted the coming of the end of the world. They're called "doomsday prophets." By contrast, I believe that the last days represent a most exciting time for the people of God. It's a time when we can expect God to do astounding things. It's a time when we will see many people reaching out to embrace the great gospel of the life, death, and resurrection of Christ Jesus our Lord.

With this great advance by the church, we can also expect a continual increase in evil. We might say it this way: as the light of the gospel of Christ shines brighter and brighter, the world of iniquity will become darker.

The Apostle Paul wrote to us the characteristics of the society and culture of the "last days" before the end of the present world and the consummation of the kingdom of God, through the coming of Christ. I believe we are given this list of characteristics for two very important reasons.

First, so that we might be aware of the times, and second, so that we will be on guard against allowing any of these characteristics to find root within us! If these kinds of attitudes and behaviors are exemplified by a world that is being consumed by ever-increasing wickedness, how much more should we, as people who claim Christ as our Lord, resist such things! Paul was saying in essence, "Pay attention! This is what the world will look like prior to the end. Make sure that you do not find yourself controlled by the same spirit, attitudes, and behaviors that you see in the world around you!"

Are we living in the "last days"? No one knows when the world will come to its final ending. We have been instructed to recognize the times, and to avoid allowing the evil of the "last days" to find root in us. I encourage you to surrender yourself afresh to Christ, our soon coming king, today!

Get Growing!

- Is your life, attitude, and behavior fully surrendered to Jesus Christ?
- How can you become more sensitive to recognize the signs of the "last days"?

Re-friending

Now I appeal to Euodia and Syntyche. Please, because you belong to the Lord, settle your disagreement.
Philippians 4:2 (NLT)

And now I want to plead with those two dear women, Euodias and Syntyche. Please, please, with the Lord's help, quarrel no more—be friends again. Philippians 4:2 (TLB)

Friends are wonderful. It's great to have people in your life that share some common connection and positive chemistry with you. Being together with a friend is something you look forward to and enjoy. You add to each other's life. Friends are a blessing and a gift.

However, sometimes friendships face challenges. Something happens in the relationship and things change. Feelings get hurt, trust is broken, motives are questioned, and communication becomes painful. Walls go up and former friends are estranged. Even worse, they become enemies.

The Apostle Paul gave a lot of attention to relationship issues in his teachings. He frequently reminded Christian believers of the traps and pitfalls of bad feelings and behavior toward one another. Sometimes he got very specific. In some situations, he even called out people by name, addressing their disagreements and division.

This was the case when he wrote to the church in a place called Philippi. Two ladies in the church who had been great friends at one time were now at odds with each other. They had an unsettled disagreement. Their disagreement had isolated them from each other and was affecting other people around them.

Paul was deeply concerned about what these ladies had allowed to come between them. If you read further in Philippians 4 you will discover that these women had once been great friends and had worked together—side-by-side—serving God and the church. Their relationship plummeted for some reason. Over time they moved from cooperating with each other to contending with each other.

What was Paul's guidance to them? He told them to "re-friend" each other. This meant that they would have to drop their offenses, whatever they were, and forgive. They had to willingly lay down their "right to be right" about their disagreement, to reconcile and move forward together again.

How about you? What friendship has dissolved because of some disagreement? Are you hurt and angry with your former friend? Have you closed your heart to that person? It's time to take a step in faith and ask the Lord for forgiveness and to heal that broken relationship. Be the one to take the first step toward "re-friending!"

Get Growing!

- Are there friendships in your life that are stressed or even broken?
- What decisions and actions do you need to take to restore and strengthen these relationships again?

Be Picky

*Become wise by walking with the wise; hang out with
fools and watch your life fall to pieces.*
Proverbs 13:20 (MSG)

*People and their lives are like trees. Good trees bear
beautiful, tasty fruit, but bad trees bear ugly, bitter fruit.
A good tree cannot bear ugly, bitter fruit; nor can a bad
tree bear fruit that is beautiful and tasty.*
Matthew 7:17-18 (Voice)

What are the most important decisions you will ever
make in life? If you believe the Bible, the answer to this
question is an easy one. Choosing to develop a personal
relationship with God is the most important thing you
could do. It's the best choice you will ever make.

But there is another choice—actually a lifelong chain of
choices you will make—that has a whole lot to do with
where you end up in life, and often, where a person ends up
eternally. It's your choice of friends. It's the decisions you
make about the people you allow into your life, and the
ones you cut out of your life. Who you hang out with and
hang around with will impact your life far more than you
can imagine. If you welcome the wrong influences and reject
the right ones, you will pay a price.

Over the years, I have watched many horror stories
unfold all because folks made bad choices about their friends
and associates. I have seen incredible potential squandered,
pure spirits poisoned, people's lives ruined, and even a few
pay the price of a shortened life all because of a lack of good
"people sense."

Lest we think that bad choices about people is an error reserved for the young, we must remember that no one is immune at any time in life from being foolish when it comes to choosing friends. There are as many foolish fifty- and sixty-year-olds as there are twenty- and thirty-year-olds. Many sad stories testify to the fact that age doesn't always guarantee wisdom.

Jesus reminded us that fruit never lies. If a tree has apples, it's an apple tree. If it produces oranges, it's an orange tree. To know what kind of tree you are dealing with, look at the fruit.

The same is true for choosing friends. *Be picky!* Before you give someone a place of influence in your life, pick some of their fruit. Watch how they live. Listen to how they talk. Tune in to what they are communicating with their spirit and attitudes. If you ever taste bad fruit, bitter fruit, bug-infested fruit—run! Look for another tree. When you find the right fruit, you have found the right tree.

Choose your friends carefully. It is one of the most important decisions you will ever make in life.

Get Growing!

- What kind of fruit are your friends and friendships yielding?
- Consider the long-lasting impact your friends will have in your life. Are you choosing them carefully?

Stay Strong and Keep Going!

*Let us not become weary in doing good, for at the
proper time we will reap a harvest if we do not give up.*
Galatians 6:9 (NIV)

One of the tendencies we all have is to quit—to give up
when the going gets tough. I have watched many people
over the years give in to the temptation to drop out of the
race, give up on solving their problems, run away from
their challenges or resign from their responsibilities because
of weariness or personal frustration. The sad thing is that
these folks were quite often on the brink of a breakthrough
and didn't realize it. Victory was only a few paces away, but
their lack of patience and persistence cost them the win.

Today's verse teaches us that when we give up
prematurely we miss the harvest God has for us. What kind
of harvest do we forfeit when we quit doing what God has
asked us to do?

We miss the harvest of personal character growth. Our
challenging times and tough situations are designed to
make us mature, strong, and useful to God at a higher and
greater level. When we bail, we delay the development God
is trying to bring to us. Just like a cake has to remain in an
oven for the right amount of time to be ready to enjoy, we
have to stay *"in the heat"* long enough for our character to
form the sweetness and richness of Jesus' life and presence.

When we give up too soon we also miss the harvest of
incredible breakthroughs. When a farmer plants a seed, he
does not expect an immediate harvest. He expects to *wait*.
His waiting is not passive, it is active. While he is waiting,
he fertilizes the plants, cultivates the crops, and keeps a

check on the weeds that would destroy his eventual harvest. He does all this believing that his efforts will bring results.

The analogy applies to us. When we faithfully and patiently continue to plant the right seeds through prayer, fasting and obedient living, and continue to cultivate this part of our lives, we can expect a payoff—a harvest—breakthroughs to come.

God's Word to us is, don't be a half-baked believer! Don't miss the breakthroughs God wants to bring to your life. Stay strong and keep going!

Get Growing!

- When was the last time you stayed strong and kept going through the heat of a situation? What changes did you see in your life? What lessons did you learn from that situation?
- Have you ever prematurely given up and missed the harvest God had for you? What lessons did you learn from that situation?
- How can you remain confident when you are waiting for the harvest?

Be Big

Even if that person wrongs you seven times a day and each time turns again and asks forgiveness, you must forgive.
Luke 17:4 (NLT)

We sometimes have needs that require us to ask someone for something. "Making the ask" for aid, assistance, or advice isn't easy for many people. While some people should be named "*Ask,*" because of the frequency and shamelessness of their requests, there are many others for whom asking anyone for anything is absolutely excruciating.

There's one kind of ask that's hard for practically everybody—asking for forgiveness. Think about the last time you realized that something you said, did, or failed to do was wrong, hurtful, disrespectful, or damaging to someone else. Maybe it was intentional. Usually it's not.

What's your normal response when you become aware of your mistakes? Is it easy or hard for you to ask for forgiveness? Are you quick or slow in seeking it? Do you blame others and make excuses for yourself, or do you humbly accept responsibility for your failures and freely admit your shortcomings promptly?

Personal growth happens when we readily apologize. Relationships are restored and strengthened when we learn to say, "*Please forgive me. I was wrong!*" Great things happen when we're quick to admit mistakes and ask for forgiveness.

What can we expect to happen when we proactively seek forgiveness?
- Our character matures.
- We learn something about the power and importance of humility.

- We develop a deeper understanding of ourselves.
- We're better able to identify personal areas of needed growth and change.
- Our relationship skills improve.

Not only does asking for forgiveness benefit us, it also helps and blesses others. It can lead to:
- The rebuilding of trust.
- The renewing of love.
- The removal of tension, animosity, and strife.
- The reconciliation of broken friendships.

Don't let your pride or procrastination stand in the way. Send the note, make the call, have the conversation. Apologize with sincerity and humility. You'll become a bigger, better person when you do.

Get Growing!

Who do you need to ask to forgive you? Decide right now that you're going to take the brave step to say, *"Please forgive me for _____. I was wrong."*

Critical Spirits

Do not judge, or you too will be judged. For in the same way you judge others, you will be judged, and with the measure you use, it will be measured to you.
Matthew 7:1-2 (NIV)

Have you ever known someone with a "critical spirit"? These are people who consistently look for and see the faults of others. Being plagued by a negative outlook, they have a need to find the foibles and failures of others. People with a "critical attitude" make others miserable!

One of the crippling problems of the church through the ages is this very problem. Nothing pleases the adversary more than stimulating and propagating a negative, critical spirit within the body of Christ. This attitude is often manifested in the critical attacks of one segment of the church against another. It is sometimes seen in church members criticizing and judging other members over issues that are insignificant. It is an attitude that promotes division and strife instead of unity and peace.

Charles Spurgeon, in his classic book, *Lectures To My Students*, comments on his encounter with this attitude in the church he pastored. He wrote, "When I came to New Park Street Chapel as a young man, I was speedily interviewed by a good man who had left the church, having, as he said, been treated shamefully. He mentioned the names of half-a-dozen people, all prominent members of the church, who had behaved in a very unchristian manner to him, he, the poor innocent sufferer, having been a model of patience and holiness. I learned his character at once from what he said about others (a mode of judging which has never misled me)..."

Mr. Spurgeon makes a very astute observation in the little story he described. What he learned and observed is important for us to understand. He said that one of the ways he learned to judge the character of people, throughout his years of ministry, was by the things they said about others. This is a powerful truth! What someone says about another person tells you more about him or her than the one they are criticizing.

Jesus taught us in Matthew 7:1-2 about the dangers and consequences of a critical and judgmental spirit. We will be judged the same way we judge.

Avoid the enemies' trap of a negative and critical attitude of others. Instead, let's learn to walk in the attributes of godly love toward others today.

Get Growing!

How frequently do you make critical or questionable statements about others? Do you enter conversations where negative statements are being made about others? How often do you judge others without knowing their hearts? Our answers to these questions reveal either the presence or absence of a critical spirit within our hearts and lives.

Got Problems?

So we don't look at the troubles we can see now; rather, we fix our gaze on things that cannot be seen. For the things we see now will soon be gone, but the things we cannot see will last forever. 2 Corinthians 4:18 (NLT)

If you were given a sheet of paper and asked to write down the top five, most troubling problems in your life currently, what would be on the list?

All of us encounter difficulties, disappointments, stress, and pain in life. Things happen to us that we do not understand. There are things that do not go according to our plans or agenda. If anyone ever had problems, the Apostle Paul certainly did.

Here are a few things he faced: *We are pressed on every side by troubles.... We are perplexed.... We are hunted down.... We get knocked down.... Through suffering.... Yes, we live under constant danger of death because we serve Jesus.... (2 Corinthians 4:8-11 NLT)*

Look at some of the words he used, "pressed," "perplexed," "hunted down," "knocked down," "suffering," "under the constant danger of death." These certainly qualify as big, serious problems.

The interesting thing about Paul is how he maintained his perspective in the face of all of his struggles. In the verse of Scripture at the top, we get to know Paul's heart and discover some of his amazing attitudes. We see the perspective he possessed when problems came his way.

Paul viewed problems as inevitable. He was not shocked by the presence of difficulties. He understood that problems and pain are simply a part of what life portions to us.

This perspective kept him from being overly disturbed or confused in his troubles.

This is an important perspective for us as well. Problems are a part of life. Life is hard at times. Our troubles, while unique to us, are not truly unique. Everybody—yes, *everybody*—has them! Knowing this helps us to think straight when they come our way.

Paul also understood that problems are temporary. They don't last. They come and they go. Even if our difficulties last a lifetime, as believers in Jesus Christ, we have the assurance of heaven, where our troubles will come to an end.

Got problems? How is your perspective? Remember, troubles are inevitable, but they are also temporary. Follow Paul's example. Look past your problems to the good that is around the corner.

Get Growing!

- What can you do to readjust your perspective of the problems you are facing?
- What did you learn from today's study that will help you do this?

Sharp Tongue

Those who control their tongue will have a long life; a quick retort can ruin everything. Proverbs 13:3 (NLT)

One of the ingredients of a successful life is keeping the right things under control. While there are many things that are outside our realm of control, or responsibility to control, there are other things that God expects us to control carefully and prudently. One of our major problems in life is that we often try to control the things we have no business controlling, and fail to control those things we should.

The Bible makes it clear that controlling our tongue—what we say and how we say it—is necessary if we are going to experience the kind of life God intends for us to have. How many of us detour, and in some cases totally destroy our lives, because we refuse to learn this lesson? Instead of carefully guarding what we say, we allow ourselves to speak unfiltered, unguarded words, and then wonder why we have so much trouble and pain.

While there are many sins of the tongue that we should be concerned about, and committed to conquering, today's verse speaks of a particular kind of verbal sin. It refers to the *"quick retort."* A retort is sharp, sarcastic, cutting, damaging words, usually spoken without consideration of the pain they may cause or the damage they may do.

Some folks are highly skilled in retorting, but all of us are prone to it. In the pressure of a moment, when we feel attacked or irritated, when we have lost our patience or feel provoked, when we are tired, frustrated or angry, we all have a tendency to say hurtful things to others. The Bible tells us that such speech can *"ruin everything."*

Have you ever had a potentially enjoyable event ruined by a few sharp words? Have you ever had a friendship wrecked because of careless, cutting remarks? Have you ever found yourself desperately trying to minimize the damage you caused to someone or some situation by regrettable comments?

All of us know the agony of wishing we had not said something; of wanting to recapture the words we let slip out of our mouth that had hurt instead of helped someone. We know, firsthand, the ruin that a retorting tongue wreaks.

The Bible tells us that all this pain can be avoided if we simply learn to control what we say. If we would discipline ourselves to think before we speak, to moderate our reactions, to pause and reflect before we retort, our lives and relationships would be so much better.

Get Growing!

- What are the events that trigger sharp words to come out your mouth?
- How can you protect and discipline yourself from making regrettable comments to someone?

Will + Power

About midnight Paul and Silas were praying and singing hymns to God.... Suddenly there was such a violent earthquake that the foundations of the prison were shaken. At once all the prison doors flew open, and everybody's chains came loose. Acts 16:25-26 (NIV)

It has been said that spiritual growth is the result of a certain kind of willpower—not the kind of willpower that reveals itself in a stiff resolve to change our personal habits and character, but another kind. It's found in the process of giving our will to God, which only we can do, followed by the release of God's power to help us grow and change, which only he can do. We might call it *will + power.*

- We give God our will, by choosing obedience to his Word, authority and rule.
- He gives us his power to obey, and changes us in the process.

In the book of Acts, we find a great story illustrating the intersection of this *will + power* process and principle. It's the account of Paul and Silas in the Philippian jail. After being severely beaten and thrown in prison because of their faith in and witness for Jesus, Paul and Silas most likely were in no mood for celebrations. Nevertheless, they chose—they exercised their wills—to do what they knew to be the right thing to do: pray and praise. This was a decision they made for themselves. In the midst of a real life test, they determined their course of action—to go to God. They exercised their wills to do God's will.

The result was astounding, incredible, amazing, awesome, and a lot of other superlatives. God's power showed up in a big way and shook everything that could be shaken. Prison doors opened, chains fell off, Paul and Silas found freedom, and the jailer met Jesus. Not bad! It all happened at the intersection of *will + power*.

We, too, need to be aware of this spiritual intersection and do what Paul and Silas did when they faced it. When we choose to align our will with God's Word and will, he shows up in power to free us, change us, deliver us, and grow us up in him. As he works *in* us by his power, he also works *through* us to reach a lost and needy world.

Give God *your* will and get ready to experience *his* power.

Get Growing!

Make this your prayer today:

Dear Lord, thank you for making your power available to me. I desperately want to experience it in my life. Forgive me for the times I've chosen to exercise my will in making decisions. Help me keep my will in line with the Bible and your will so that I can truly know your power. In Jesus' name, Amen."

A Giant

As soon as the Israelite army saw him, they began to
run away in fright. "Have you seen the giant?" the men
asked. "He comes out each day to defy Israel."
1 Samuel 17:24-25 (NLT)

Almost everybody knows the classic Bible story about
David and Goliath. This happens at a time when the
Philistines were challenging Israel's army. Goliath, the giant
Philistine champion, stopped Israel's army. For forty days,
Goliath loomed over Israel's warriors, paralyzing them with
fear. A big man with a big mouth had taken control of God's
people. No one was willing to fight the giant. All of Israel's
soldiers were emotionally locked down, living in retreat. A
giant dominated their lives and threatened their future.

The picture of Israel's army in this pitiful state is one that
hits close to home. If we could see inside each other—if we
could know what's really going on in heads and hearts—we
would see people all around us who are frozen, paralyzed,
intimidated, living under the control of some kind of a *giant*.
If we're honest with ourselves, we'd see a few giants that are
controlling us, too.

Every time we build up enough courage, fortitude, guts,
faith to go after our giant, he roars out in his intimidating
voice, with his giant-sized spirit, breathing out his hateful,
demonic, vile threats. We're paralyzed!

Our giants tell us there's no way to conquer them. We're
told that we'll be a victim, a captive, prey, for the rest of our
lives. They tell us that we should never dream of victory.
They want us to submit to their domination and control.
They push us into a corner and demand that we live there,

in a restricted place and limited space. These giants slowly drain our hope and faith, our passion, our resolve to fight. Before long, we're totally convinced that what the giant says is true. We're done.

The beauty of this Bible story is that it doesn't end in defeat. It ends with an incredible victory. What everyone thought couldn't happen, *happened*. The giant was confronted and conquered. The thing that no one thought was possible became possible because of one man's willingness to step up and address this big bully.

A young man named David not only stepped onto a battlefield that day, but onto the stage of history. He showed us that there are battles that, although big, are worth fighting. David taught us that our size, our weapons, and our limitations don't matter when we're fighting the right battles, because Almighty God fights for people who trust in him. He fights for people who are willing to confront the evil, dark, intimidating forces that have paralyzed them.

Get Growing!

- What giants have appeared in your life to intimidate and paralyze you?
- How has reading this passage adjusted your perspective about dealing with the giants in your life?

How Can We Reduce Our Regrets?

So the Israelites examined their food, but they did not consult the Lord. Joshua 9:14 (NLT)

Have you ever made a decision that you later regretted? Sure, everyone has made bad decisions. Too often, we look back over our lives and see that a little more patience and a lot more listening to and obeying God's Word would have helped us avoid mistakes and the ugly messes we have gotten ourselves into.

Many lessons in Scripture remind us of the importance of relying on God in the process of our daily decision-making, such as the story of the Gibeonites. In today's passage, God had instructed the people of Israel to conquer the idolatrous people living in the Promised Land. Israel experienced miraculous victories at two Canaanite cities, Jericho and Ai. When a neighboring nation called the Gibeonites heard about Israel's victorious invasion, they were terrified. They decided that their best protection was to establish a peace treaty with the people of God. So, they fabricated a story and enacted a drama about traveling from a distant country, to convince Joshua that they were not residents of Canaan, and gain Israel's mercy to avoid attack.

The Gibeonites arrived at Israel's camp and presented their story to Joshua and Israel's leaders. The Israelites examined the outward evidence—the moldiness of their food and deterioration of their supplies—all a ruse the Gibeonites had created. From this outward observation, Joshua and his leaders drew the conclusion that the Gibeonites were telling the truth. They entered into a peace treaty with them.

Israel's leaders never asked God for his wisdom and insight. They relied on their own capacities for evaluating the situation. Deceived through their own self-reliance, they entered into a relationship with a group of idolatrous people that God intended for them to destroy. Once the treaty was made, they could not back out (Joshua 9:1-15).

What a warning and lesson this is for us. We get into all kinds of trouble, wrong relationships, bad agreements and partnerships, when we make evaluations like the Israelites did. We tend to view and assess circumstances with our natural eyes, human reasoning, and independent thinking. We make decisions that seem right, reasonable, and advantageous. Often we don't consult God, or else consult him only casually. We walk through life trusting our own limited wisdom and insight, rather than tapping into the wisdom of the all-wise God. The result is a lot of unnecessary pain, problems, and regret.

How can we reduce regrets? We can never live completely regret-free, but we can reduce regrets by regularly going to God for wisdom, and patiently waiting upon him for his insights and perspective. We can learn to consult him rather than rely on our own limited knowledge. When you ask God for wisdom and wait on him for it, you can be sure that he will give it to you.

Get Growing!

- What steps can you take to reduce regret in your life?
- Think of a time when you made a regrettable decision. What consequences did you face?

Cleaning Out

Guard your heart more than anything else, because the source of your life flows from it. Proverbs 4:23 (GW)

The human heart is much like a container. Throughout life we accumulate experiences and emotions, some good and some not so good. The good times and relationships of life leave us with positive memories and pleasant feelings. They build trust in us, and bring us joy and positive expectations for the future.

The painful experiences of life can also leave marks on our souls. They often deposit in us an ugly residue of anger, bitterness and resentment. They can rob us of hope and happiness. They can distort our perspective of people and circumstances. They can lead us to bad decisions, bad thinking, and dominating, destructive life habits.

In the passage above, we see a sobering reminder that what we accumulate inside us affects everything outside us. That's why it's important to check and clean out the contents of our hearts. It's vital that we know what we've allowed to occupy space in our souls, and to actively address the things that are poisonous and painful.

How do we do this? Here are some key steps:

- Understand the negative consequences of allowing the wrong things to take up space in your heart.
- Ask God to help you identify the things that need to be removed from your heart.
- Ask God to cleanse your heart of everything that has contaminated you.

- Ask God to heal any brokenness and pain in your heart.
- Choose to forgive anyone and everyone who has caused problems and pain in your life.
- Develop filters for your heart and mind that keep the bad out and let only the good in.

The contents of your heart matters. What is there affects all your thoughts, choices, attitudes, and actions. Don't let the wrong things accumulate inside of you. Decide to clean out the poison and pain from your heart, and ask God to help you keep your heart free and clean from everything that might contaminate it. It's one of the best decisions you'll ever make, and one of the most important prayers you'll ever pray!

Get Growing!

- Take time to search your heart and identify the things that need to be removed and cleansed out.
- What steps will you take to put a filter to your heart to protect it from poisonous things?

Priorities

Remember the Sabbath day by keeping it holy. Six days
you shall labor and do all your work, but the seventh day
is a Sabbath to the Lord your God.
Exodus 20:8-10 (NIV)

Have you ever felt as though your life was coming apart
at the seams?

One of the major struggles of life involves maintaining
proper priorities. We so easily allow our lives to become
unbalanced. When our lives are unbalanced, we become
unhealthy and unproductive.

Our lives become unbalanced at times when we embrace
the wrong priorities. Wrong priorities lead to a wrong
investment of our life resources. When we maintain the
right priorities, we can invest our energies into those things
that result in peaceful and healthy life.

In the Ten Commandments, we find an instruction given
to us that is actually designed to assist us in maintaining
proper priorities. In the fourth commandment, God defines
for us three of the most important priorities that we are to
maintain in our lives. Embracing these priorities will lead to
a productive, fulfilling, and healthy life.

The first priority given by God is the "priority of
worship." God gave the Sabbath to mankind for the
purpose of corporate worship. God says in essence, "Make
corporate worship a priority in your life. Schedule this into
your week." When we fail to do this, we become spiritually
weak and vulnerable. But when we establish this priority,
we find renewed spiritual strength and wholeness.

The second priority established by God in this commandment is the "priority of work." As surely as we are commanded to worship, we are commanded to work. Our worship gives focus to our work. Regular worship leads us to revitalized work. Work has been the target of "bad press." Contrary to what some Christians think, work is not the result of the fall of man. Man was given the responsibility of work *prior* to the fall. God values work. He has established it as a priority for our lives.

The third priority found in the fourth commandment is the "priority of restoration." We need regular physical restoration. We need times of spiritual, mental, and emotional restoration, and times to restore our relationships. The basic meaning of the word "Sabbath" is "rest."

The Sabbath is much more than a particular day of the week; it is a way of living! Let's commit to prioritizing rest every day.

Get Growing!

- Are you obeying the fourth commandment by maintaining the proper priorities in your life?
- What steps can you take to faithfully remember the principles of Sabbath Day and apply them to your daily walk?

Valuables and Assets

So it is right that I should feel as I do about all of you, for you have a special place in my heart. You share with me the special favor of God, both in my imprisonment and in defending and confirming the truth of the Good News. God knows how much I love you and long for you with the tender compassion of Christ Jesus.
Philippians 1:7-8 (NLT)

A "valuable" is something we consider to have great worth—something we highly esteem and seek to protect, something we give top priority to and hold as extremely important.

An "asset" is a resource for meeting needs or accomplishing goals. The word comes from an old French term which means, "enough" or "satisfied." Based on this definition, an asset is something that gives us a sense of security and satisfaction about our life. It's something that gives us meaning and worth. It's something we hold on to for identity—the thing or things that make us feel like we are enough.

Many people think of valuables and assets as "stuff"— the material things they possess, their net worth on a balance sheet, their jewelry, automobiles, antiques, or collectibles. The security and self-worth of many folks are built on these temporal things. Ironically, when this is our understanding, our mindset creates a nagging drive to get more. Enough "stuff" is never enough to completely secure and satisfy us.

The true valuable things in life are not things at all. Our real assets are not material or measurable on a balance sheet. The most valuable things in life and the greatest assets in life are relationships—our relationship with God and our relationships with people.

When I think of what is really valuable to me, when I measure the real assets of my life, I first think of Jesus and my personal relationship with him. I think of my wonderful wife and family. I think of my church family and the friends God has given me. These relationships are what make my life truly secure and satisfying.

When Paul wrote a letter to his fellow believers in the church at Philippi, he was a Roman prisoner, incarcerated for preaching the Gospel. All material things had been stripped from him, and we see what he truly valued, what he considered to be his real assets. Paul knew that life is all about relationships—our relationship with God and others.

Get Growing!

- What are the most valuable assets of your life?
- Take some time this week to let people know how much you love and appreciate them. Write an encouraging note, send an affirming email, or make an appreciative phone call.

The Joy of Giving

In everything I did, I showed you that by this kind of hard work we must help the weak, remembering the words the Lord Jesus himself said: "It is more blessed to give than to receive." Acts 20:35 (NIV)

The best decisions in life are made when we live by the right principles. While emotions often mislead us, right principles never will.

Paul reminds us of a life principle given to us by Jesus— the "giving principle." It's a truth that is a guide and direct us in all our decisions. According to numerous studies, people who give generously and regularly are happier, healthier, and less stressed. They report a greater sense of meaning and purpose in life. And, they live more impacting lives.

I am convinced this is a major reason that God gave the commandment of tithing. His command to return the first ten percent of what he has provided to us gets us started on the pathway of giving. He commands us to do this so that we cannot excuse ourselves from the giving act. He knows that once we start giving, we will forever be hooked on it and blessed by it.

"Bring the whole tithe into the storehouse, that there may be food in my house. Test me in this," says the Lord Almighty, "and see if I will not throw open the floodgates of heaven and pour out so much blessing that you will not have room enough for it" Malachi 3:10 (NIV).

Tithing brings blessings. In research comparing people who tithed to those who didn't, the tithing group was healthier and stronger in every one of nine areas studied.

There is great joy in giving. Here are five ways to experience the joy of giving:

- Believe in the life principle of giving. Accept as a true-life principle that "it is more blessed to give than to receive."
- Obey it personally. Let generosity become a practice and guiding principle in your life. Many people talk about faith and doing something great for God, yet fail to practice giving. Consistent giving proves real faith more than anything else.
- Give for the right reasons. Give to honor God, to advance his church and kingdom, and to be a blessing.
- Give wholeheartedly and holistically. Be cheerful when you give. Don't give grudgingly or in part. Embrace the principle in all areas—your time, treasure and talents.
- Keep growing as a giver. Do not continue to live at the same giving level. Enlarge and increase your faith by expanding your giving.

We are never more like God than when we give!

Get Growing!

Are you being consistent with your tithing to God? If not, how can you grow in giving? God gave us many resources we can give, such as time, love, and money.

"Disappointments" or "His-appointments"

How long must I make decisions alone with sorrow in my heart day after day? How long will my enemy triumph over me? Psalm 13:2 (GW)

We have all experienced...

- someone that failed to keep an important promise to us.
- someone we were relying on that did not come through.
- something we hoped for or dreamed about that did not happen.
- an expectation we had that was unfulfilled or under-fulfilled.

If we are not careful, the frustration and pain of disappointment can become deadly. It can ignite anger or invite despair. Over time, accumulated disappointments can make people bitter, brittle, or make them retreat into cynicism where they trust almost no one or nothing.

A change of perspective can help you turn your disappointments into "his-appointments!" It allows you to see your disappointments in the light of God's wisdom, grace and providence.

Here's how to turn disappointments into "his-appointments":

1. Remember that everyone experiences disappointments.

When you are disappointed, it is easy to convince yourself that you are the victim of a horrible cosmic plan specifically designed to make you, and you only, miserable. "The universe is picking on me!" In reality, disappointment is a part of life. Accept it. Embrace it. Expect it. God never promised you a disappointment-free life. Everybody has disappointments.

2. Look for important life lessons.

What can you learn from a disappointment that will make you a better person? How can a disappointment help you avoid being a disappointment to others? What character or personality issues did a disappointment reveal in your life? What life principles will you take away from the experience that will make you wiser?

3. Trust God to work out his plan.

Believe in the almighty, all-powerful, all wise, all good, all loving, God of the Bible who said that for you: *"all things are possible,"* and *"nothing is too hard for me."* Embrace that God is able to handle the disappointments that come. Disappointments do not intimidate God or jeopardize his plans. Often the disappointments we are upset about are God's ways of getting our attention and adjusting our life course. Do not live in disappointment. Turn your disappointments into "his-appointments."

Get Growing!

- What character or personality issues are revealed to you in moments of disappointment?
- In what ways, have you allowed disappointments to hinder your life, relationships and walk with the Lord?

Wait Patiently

But they that wait upon the Lord shall renew their strength. They shall mount up with wings like eagles; they shall run and not be weary; they shall walk and not faint.
Isaiah 40:31 (TLB)

Patient endurance is what you need now, so that you will continue to do God's will. Then you will receive all that he has promised. Hebrews 10:36 (NLT)

If you've ever been with kids on a road trip you know that at some point on the journey, you'll hear the question, *"Are we there yet?"* When the answer is, *"No,"* the follow-up is, *"How much longer till we get there?"*

Adults aren't much different. We want to *get there*—wherever "there" is—as quickly as possible. In general, people don't like things that require waiting. We want to be there *now.*

Often, we're so busy worrying about reaching our goals and achieving our dreams that we miss the joy of the journey that takes us to them. The fact is, most worthwhile things in life take time to materialize and realize. Reaching a meaningful life destination usually involves a journey. Waiting is part of the process.

Since we have to wait, we would benefit from some *"wait*-training," so we can wait well. The best way to wait is patiently. Of course the opposite of waiting patiently is to wait impatiently. It really does no good, because either way—*you wait!*

When we wait well, good things happen. Here's how to be a patient *waiter:*

P = Pray. Use wait time as prayer time.

A = Apply yourself diligently and faithfully to your present assignments and opportunities.

T = Trust God with your future. His plans may be different from your plans, but they're always better than your plans.

I = Identify and Invest in areas of your character that need attention.

E = Enjoy the journey. The journey is not only necessary, it's valuable.

N = Nix the Negatives. Don't give room to grumbling.

T = Be thankful. Live with a spirit of gratitude. Praise and thank God for who he is, what he's done, what he's doing, and what he's going to do!

Get Growing!

- Are you a patient or impatient waiter?
- How can you become a patient waiter in all areas of your life?

Tackling Tough Times

Even when I walk through the darkest valley, I will not be afraid, for you are close beside me. Your rod and your staff protect and comfort me. Psalm 23:4 (NLT)

The late Dr. Robert Schuller wrote a book entitled, *Tough Times Never Last, But Tough People Do*. What a terrific title! In that one short, powerful phrase, we are reminded of two key principles:

- Life problems and challenges are temporary.
- People with the right qualities can outlast and overcome the toughest of times.

Tough times come to us all. No one is immune from seasons of difficulty and periods of pressure. As believers, we face testing and trials of our faith. In some moments, life throws us painful shots. On some mornings, instead of enthusiastically getting up to face the world, we would prefer to pull the cover over our heads and hide.

While tough times come, they don't come to stay. They come for a while, and then are on their way. Understanding the temporary nature of tough times is one of the keys to getting through them.

In this passage, David reminds us that God intends to get us through our dark valleys, not leave us in them. Dark valleys are never meant to be our dwelling place. Tough times never last. Life problems and challenges come only for a season.

But tough people with the right qualities can endure and overcome the toughest of times. We can build qualities into our lives that will make us appropriately tough on the inside—tough enough to handle the testing and trials of our faith.

Toughness should not be confused with callousness. God wants us to have a tender heart along with a tough, enduring commitment to press through our challenging and difficult seasons. This kind of toughness involves an inner resolve, a determined faith, a persistent hope, and a dedicated faithfulness. It involves a consistency of life that outlasts and overcomes whatever tough times we may be facing.

Remember, any tough times you are going through right now are temporary. Keep your heart tender and your spirit strong. Walk *through* your valley, don't set up camp there! God helps us to have a tender heart along with a tough, enduring commitment to press through our challenging and difficult seasons.

Get Growing!

- Are you going through a tough time right now? What are some qualities we must have to overcome the toughest of times?
- How can you develop and apply those qualities in your life or use them to encourage someone else?

Doubt

But now be strong, O Zerubbabel, declares the Lord.
Be strong, O Joshua son of Jozadak, the high priest.
Be strong, all you people of the land, declares the
Lord, and work. For I am with you, declares the Lord
Almighty. Haggai 2:4 (NIV)

One of the most debilitating diseases of the Christian life is that of chronic doubt. It attacks our faith, hinders our spiritual progress, and leaves us depressed and discouraged.

The prophet Haggai addressed the problem of chronic doubt among the people of God. The Jews had been released from their Babylonian exile by Cyrus, King of Persia. Fifty thousand had returned from Babylon to Jerusalem to rebuild the temple that had been destroyed by Nebuchadnezzar. The rebuilding was riddled with obstacles, problems, and chronic doubt. As the temple was being rebuilt, doubts arose about succeeding because of the economic crisis they were facing.

But there was also another issue that generated doubt. Some of the older builders were discouraged because they had seen Solomon's Temple before it was destroyed. They compared the new temple to the magnificence of the old one. The builders were negatively influenced by their perspectives of the past.

In the same way, our perspectives of the past can rob us of faith for the present and future. Some individuals spend great amounts of time and energy regretting their past. This breeds condemnation, judgment, and resentment. It opens the door to doubts about one's ability to succeed in the present. On the other hand, some people idolize the past. They live in the "good old days." This is exactly what happened to these builders in Jerusalem.

God sent an instructional word to them: *"But now be strong, O Zerubbabel, declares the Lord. Be strong, O Joshua son of Jozadak, the high priest. Be strong, all you people of the land, declares the Lord, and work. For I am with you, declares the Lord Almighty"* (Haggai 2:4).

Then, he exhorted them to renewed faith with this great promise, *"The glory of the present house will be greater than the glory of the former house, says the Lord Almighty. And in this place I will grant peace, declares the Lord Almighty"* (Haggai 2:9).

God is saying to us in essence, "Don't let regrets or idolization of the past rob you of faith for the present and future. Get busy working, get busy believing, because the best is yet to come!"

Get Growing!

- Are you paralyzed in your life by chronic doubt?
- Are your memories of the past keeping you from investing in the present? Renew your faith. Let go of the past and embrace all that God has for you!

Honest to God

Repent and live. Ezekiel 18:32 (NIV)

Son of man, give your people this message: The righteous behavior of righteous people will not save them if they turn to sin, nor will the wicked behavior of wicked people destroy them if they repent and turn from their sins.
Ezekiel 33:12 (NLT)

I enjoy reading the Old Testament books of Isaiah, Jeremiah, and Ezekiel. God used each of these prophets to address the sins of his people and to warn them of impending and imminent judgment. Their messages were blunt, strong, and sobering.

As I have waded through the pages of these books, I have tried to answer a key question—what is the central theme? What is the "take away" from these very serious warnings and messages by three deeply committed and passionate prophets of God?

The theme is clearly revealed in Ezekiel's words in the verse of Scripture above, *"Repent and live!"* The whole focus of the prophets' messages was about bringing people to repentance. God is a gracious and forgiving God. He responds to repentance. Repentance attracts God's mercy. One of the greatest qualities we can develop is to be quick to repent.

Repentance involves feeling sorry for our sins. It involves brokenness and contriteness of heart. It involves being aware of and deeply grieved over ugly parts of our personal character. Real repentance involves action. Repentant people change. The clear sign that we have repented of something is a changed heart, changed attitudes, and changed behavior.

To get to this wonderful point called repentance requires honesty. We have to be honest with ourselves and with God. We must own responsibility for our sins and failures instead of justifying them, rationalizing them or blaming them on others. This kind of honesty with ourselves and with God is painful. While it hurts, it also prepares us to experience the hope of change.

God will do great things in us and through us when a true spirit of repentance is present in our hearts. Repentance releases life!

Get Growing!

- What are some things you need to repent of today?
- Here is a simple prayer of confession and repentance to God. Mediate deeply through your life before praying.

"Father in heaven, I am deeply sorry for _____. I realize that my actions were sinful and they are not in accordance to your Word and what you want for my life. Father, I ask for the forgiveness of my sins and restoration of my heart. In Jesus' Name, Amen!"

One Thing I Do Know

"Is this your son?" they asked. "Is this the one you say was born blind? How is it that now he can see?" "We know he is our son," the parents answered, "and we know he was born blind. But how he can see now, or who opened his eyes, we don't know. Ask him. He is of age; he will speak for himself." ...A second time they summoned the man who had been blind. "Give glory to God by telling the truth," they said. "We know this man is a sinner." He replied, "Whether he is a sinner or not, I don't know. One thing I do know. I was blind but now I see!"
John 9:19-25 (NIV)

In the story of Jesus' personal ministry to a man who was born blind, Jesus reached out and gave the man his sight. Jesus gave the man access to a world he had never known. He was able to see and experience life in beautiful images and color. The man was obviously thrilled. All his family, friends, and neighbors were amazed. They wanted to know how this miracle happened. The man told them that Jesus had done this for him.

When the Pharisees, the religious leaders of the day, heard that the man was giving glory, honor, and credit to Jesus, they were concerned. They didn't want anything to diminish or undermine their role and prestige in the minds of people. These small-minded, ritual-oriented men began interrogating the man who had been healed. Instead of celebrating his healing, their goal was to discredit Jesus. Instead of rejoicing in a man's newfound life, they were only interested in protecting their image and their turf.

The Pharisees asked how he received his sight. He pointed to Jesus. The Pharisees then accused Jesus of being a sinner because he performed this miracle on the Sabbath. Then they asked the man his opinion about Jesus. The man's response was wise, powerful, and applicable to us. He cut to the bottom line. There were many things he did not know, but there was one thing he was absolutely sure of. Once he was blind, now he could see, and the One who made this possible was Jesus.

Let's look at two key thoughts from this passage:

- Jesus wants to do something in each of us that opens our eyes to a world we have never known before.
- The most effective testimony of Jesus' power that we can communicate to others is a changed life.

Ask Jesus to open your spiritual eyes to a new world you have never known before—the beautiful world of his Word and will. Let him change your life in such a wonderful way that your transformation will be an unmistakable testimony to his greatness and power.

Get Growing!

Think about areas of spiritual blindness that affect your life. How would your life be different if you would receive sight?

Guarding Against Jealousy

Anger is cruel, and wrath is like a flood, but jealousy is even more dangerous. Proverbs 27:4 (NLT)

For jealousy and selfishness are not God's kind of wisdom. Such things are earthly, unspiritual, and demonic. James 3:15 (NLT)

One of the most destructive forces in people's lives is jealousy. Think about some of the people in the Bible who were damaged or destroyed by it:

- Cain killed Abel, partly because of jealousy (Genesis 4:3-8).
- Joseph's brothers sold him into slavery because of jealousy (Genesis 37:11).
- Korah, Dathan, and Abiram were put to death because of their jealously toward Moses and their spiritual poison of God's people (Numbers 16).

Think about all the emotional energy that is expended, all the hatred that is spawned, and all the relationships that are ripped apart because of jealousy. Think about the sibling rivalries, the office politics, the envy that breed distance between people, and the inner turmoil and pain that jealousy causes. This is a high price to pay for something that brings nothing but negativity and destruction into our lives.

I have seen jealousy ruin some potentially great people by turning them into small-minded, unproductive, bitter people. I have watched disorder and evil spring up in families, businesses, friendships, and even churches when someone gave a place in their heart to jealousy.

The bad news is: All of us are vulnerable to this spirit. The good news is: God can help us avoid and overcome it. Here is help to steer clear of jealousy, or clean it out if we are infected by it:

- Own up to jealousy and confess it to God as sin. Don't justify it.
- Stop comparing yourself and your circumstances with others. Comparisons always deceive us. Things look better, fairer, greater for others than for us. Remember, "The grass is always greener on the other side!"
- Begin practicing gratitude. One of the greatest antidotes for the poison of jealousy is to purposefully count our blessings and openly express our gratitude to God and others for them.
- Do good to those you feel jealous toward. Force yourself to do and say nice things to others. You will be amazed at how these actions will counter-attack jealousy in your heart.
- Stay alert to signs of jealousy in your heart. Jealousy is subtle. When we observe distance in our relationships, disorder in our interactions, or anger in our hearts, it is time to find out what's behind these reactions. One possibility is jealousy.

Ask God to help you live a jealous-free life!

Get Growing!

Make it a priority in your spiritual growth to identify jealousy patterns in your life. Prayerfully ask God to help you overcome those patterns.

Passionate

It was time for the annual Passover celebration, and Jesus went to Jerusalem. In the Temple area he saw merchants selling cattle, sheep, and doves for sacrifices; and he saw dealers at tables exchanging foreign money. Jesus made a whip from some ropes and chased them all out of the Temple. He drove out the sheep and oxen, scattered the moneychangers' coins over the floor, and turned over their tables. Then, going over to the people who sold doves, he told them, 'Get these things out of here. Don't turn my Father's house into a marketplace!'" John 2:13-16 (NLT)

Passion is an interesting and versatile word. It's used to describe crimes committed in the heat and intensity of emotion—crimes of passion. It's also used to describe our affection or strong feelings for anything from food to hobbies, to strong personal opinions and beliefs. We often hear people say, "I'm passionate about...!"

Passion is important. It determines our priorities and pursuits. It influences our choices and actions. It generates inspiration and investment. The presence of passion can be a great blessing and its absence a terrible curse. Pure and good passions are invaluable. They are a key to a productive and fulfilled life. Polluted passions are dangerous and destructive, to us and to others. For our passions to be pure, they must be properly checked and filtered by God, his Word, and his Holy Spirit. The right passions are those that are in sync with the passions of God's heart.

Yes, God is a passionate God. There are certain things that are near and dear to his heart—things he passionately cares about. One of the best ways to determine God's passion is by looking at the life and ministry of his Son, Jesus Christ.

When we look at the life of Jesus, we discover a number of things that were very important to him. Throughout his ministry we find moments when Jesus' intensity of feelings brought to light the passions of God's heart.

Jesus had a passion for God's house. His passion revealed God's deep love for his house. What is God's house in today's world? God's house is his church, his people. God is passionate about building, strengthening, unifying, and sanctifying his people—the church. He cares deeply about our love for and involvement in his church. He wants us to share his passion for his house!

Get Growing!

- Are you passionate about connecting with and investing in building, strengthening, and unifying God's house—his church?
- How can you make this become one of your primary passions in life?

A Sincere Faith

I have been reminded of your sincere faith which first lived in your grandmother Lois and in your mother Eunice and, I am persuaded, now lives in you. 2 Timothy 1:5 (NIV)

A person who is truly sincere is a rare find in our media-oriented, cosmetic culture. Many of us may sign our letters "sincerely," but few ever stop to ask exactly what the word means.

In his second letter to Timothy, the Apostle Paul commented on a characteristic he observed in Timothy's life, which was also evident in Timothy's family. Paul declared that Timothy possessed a "sincere faith."

The Greek word found here signifies a faith that is "without hypocrisy." The word for "sincere" indicates acting or speaking with integrity, without wavering or deceit, having genuine motives. In Latin, "sincere" means "without wax." Its literal meaning in Greek is "sun-tested." It refers to a time in earlier days when men perfected creating very fine porcelain that was very expensive. When the porcelain was fired in the kiln, small cracks would sometimes appear. These small cracks reduced the value and desirability of the product. Some merchants who sold the porcelain products would resort to dishonest means of disguising and concealing the cracks. They would fill the cracks with white wax and then attempt to sell it as fine porcelain. The only way one could determine if the product was unadulterated was to hold it up to the light of the sun. Honest merchants soon began to mark their fine products "sincere," or, "without wax."

Often in our Christian journey, we are tempted to cosmetically cover over the flaws of our lives. We do all the right spiritual things externally—we go to church, we sing the hymns, we smile our religious smiles, we may even give in the offering, yet inwardly we are not living in right relationship or close communion with God. We use the wax of religion, the wax of good works to cover and conceal the real status of our spiritual condition.

When the Apostle Paul spoke of Timothy's "sincere faith" he was saying that he had carefully observed Timothy's life and there was no "wax" to be found, no hypocrisy. Timothy's faith and relationship with God was genuine.

Get Growing!

- Think of a time when you were covering yourself with wax, rather than working on your spiritual condition. What could you do to remove the wax?
- Say a prayer today asking God to help you be a sincere Christian, without wax or hypocrisy.

The Art of Asking

"Ask and it will be given to you." Matthew 7:7 (NIV)

Here I am, a stranger and a foreigner among you. Please sell me a piece of land so I can give my wife a proper burial. Genesis 23:4 (NLT)

Many things in life only come to people who ask. According to the Bible, asking is a good thing. Jesus said, *"Ask and you will receive."* It's important not to speed past that first word, *ask*. Jesus taught us that *receiving* is linked to *requesting*.

Lots of things are withheld from us when we don't ask, or when we don't know how to ask. There are right and wrong ways to ask, good and bad ways to ask, better and best ways to ask. We can "be" and "do" things that make our asking more fruitful.

In the passage above, Abraham asked some people for something. His wife Sarah had died and he wanted to bury her in an honorable tomb. He needed the right place, but the place he wanted was owned by someone who didn't seem interested in selling it. But, Abraham asked. And he received what he requested.

When you read the passage from the Book of Genesis, you will see four lessons about the right way to make a request for something:

- Ask respectfully. Abraham was very respectful and honoring in the way he made his request. His respectful attitude in asking was genuine and sincere, not manipulative.

- Ask specifically. Abraham asked with clarity and specificity. He had thought about what he wanted and needed as a proper burial place for Sarah, and he asked accordingly.
- Ask selflessly. Abraham's request was really about honoring Sarah, not satisfying some ambition for himself. The best asks happen when our requests are motivated by something other than selfish ambition. When our requests come from a desire to honor God and serve others, they are a lot more effective. Ask selflessly, not selfishly.
- Be prepared to pay the price that is required. Abraham was not making an "I want something for nothing" request. He knew that the land and tomb he wanted for his wife's gravesite would cost him something, He was ready to pay the price. Many people want something for nothing. They are only looking for what they can get out of a situation, not what they can give. Many great requests are denied because the asker is not willing to pay the price required. Abraham anted up. He paid the price, and he did so gladly.

The right kind of asking is key to receiving. To be fruitful when making requests, follow Abraham's example.

Get Growing!

Is there anything you would like to ask God? If so, spend a few minutes making your request known in a respectful, specific, and selfless way!

From Lack to Plenty

*When the master of ceremonies tasted the water that was
now wine, not knowing where it had come from (though,
of course, the servants knew), he called the bridegroom
over. "A host always serves the best wine first," he said.
"Then, when everyone has had a lot to drink, he brings
out the less expensive wine. But you have kept the best
until now!" This miraculous sign at Cana in Galilee was
the first time Jesus revealed his glory. And his disciples
believed in him. John 2:9-11(NLT)*

The first actions taken by a person appointed to a
position of authority or leadership says a lot about their
nature, character, priorities, and plans. The Apostle John
records the very first miracle Jesus performed during his
earthly ministry. It's the story of Jesus turning water into
wine at a wedding in Cana of Galilee.

Have you ever wondered why Jesus chose this as his first
"official" miracle? What does it teach us about his nature,
character, priorities, and plans?

This miracle is not really about wine or weddings. It's
about something much deeper—something Jesus wants to
communicate to each of us about his love and care.

In this story, Jesus was approached with a need. The
supply of wine for the wedding guests was depleted. People
were facing lack. What the master of the banquet originally
thought would be enough was not enough after all. Jesus
stepped into the situation, gave clear instructions, took
specific action, and the lack turned to plenty—from no
wine at all to approximately 180 gallons of wine. That's the
definition of plenty. The lack was addressed.

Also, the Lord used *ordinary* water to make *extraordinary* wine. Something common became special. When Jesus' directions were followed, water was transformed into something much more substantial and powerful.

This first miracle of Jesus reminds us that Jesus cares deeply about any kind of lack in our lives. When he is invited into situations of lack, he demonstrates his power and glory through miraculous provision. And, he specializes in taking our ordinary lives and transforming them into something extraordinary.

As you seek the Lord, bring him your lack and exchange it, by faith, for his plenty. Bring him your ordinary life and expect him to do something extraordinary in you.

Get Growing!

- Do you seek the Lord when you lack something?
- What have you been lacking that you can bring to the Lord in exchange for something greater?

Strategic Living

The boys grew up, and Esau became a skillful hunter, a man of the open country, while Jacob was a quiet man, staying among the tents. Isaac, who had a taste for wild game, loved Esau, but Rebekah loved Jacob. Once when Jacob was cooking some stew, Esau came in from the open country, famished. He said to Jacob, "Quick, let me have some of that red stew! I'm famished!" (That is why he was also called Edom.) Jacob replied, "First sell me your birthright." "Look, I am about to die," Esau said. "What good is the birthright to me?" But Jacob said, "Swear to me first." So he swore an oath to him, selling his birthright to Jacob. Then Jacob gave Esau some bread and some lentil stew. He ate and drank, and then got up and left. So Esau despised his birthright. Genesis 25:27-34 (NIV)

Certain board games are very good at teaching us how to think strategically. Checkers are less sophisticated, intellectually challenging, and time consuming than chess, but still requires strategic thinking. Checkers or chess winners think through the positive and negative implications of their moves before they make them. They are always several steps down the road in their minds. They know where they are going and how they are going to get there. Each move is weighed against the desired end result.

What is strategic thinking? Thinking is strategic when it goes after long-term goals and advances. Thinking is strategic when it focuses on a bigger picture, a greater purpose, and a positive plan for the future.

The opposite of strategic thinking is short-term thinking. Short-term thinkers yield to the wants, desires, and pressures of the immediate at the expense of the important. They do not invest spiritual, mental, and emotional effort in considering the implications of their decisions, actions, or attitudes for the future—their future.

One of the saddest examples of non-strategic thinking is seen in the Biblical story of Esau. His short-term mindset cost him his destiny. Esau's failure should cause us to stop and think about the way we are living. All of us sacrifice certain possibilities and potential for our tomorrows when we fail to think and live strategically today.

Living strategically starts with a goal. In the personal realm, it involves identifying and defining the kind of person we want to become in character and skill in the next one, five, or ten years, and setting in motion the decisions and disciplines required to get us there. It involves getting rid of habits, behaviors, and attitudes that are robbing us of our spiritual, mental, emotional, and relational potential, no matter how deep-seated they are or how comfortable we are with them.

Set some goals and enjoy the rewards of living strategically!

Get Growing!

- Do you plan your future strategically? How would you benefit from strategic thinking?
- Have you ever identified what kind of person you want to become in the next one, five and ten years?

How to Keep a Good Attitude

You must have the same attitude that Christ Jesus had.
Philippians 2:5 (NLT)

Attitudes affect our feelings, impact our productivity, and determine the quality of our relationships. We should never underestimate the power of attitude. When attitudes are improved, all parts of our lives improve.

An attitude is just the way we think about something or someone, and the emotions that go along with these thoughts. Attitudes are carried inside, but are projected outside to the people around us. They spill out through words, tones, and actions. Attitudes always come out. Good or bad, they always leak into our interactions and conversations.

Attitudes are never neutral in their impact. They prompt a response or reaction from others. They can build up or tear down, bless or curse, strengthen or weaken, lighten or weigh down, bring peace or produce pressure, unify or divide. Attitudes saturate people and places, change them for better or worse, and can be contagious.

Positive attitudes produce a positive atmosphere. Everyone enjoys an environment where people have positive attitudes. Life, relationships, momentum, and morale improve significantly when attitudes improve.

Because attitudes are so powerful, Satan works hard to soil and sour them. One bad attitude goes a long way. How many days are ruined, how much productivity is lost, how much pain is caused, all because of one person spilling contaminated attitudes on others? Here are five simple ways to keep good attitudes:

1. Set a goal to be a person that is known for incredibly good and positive attitudes. Do you want to be known as a complaining, grumbling, discontented, divisive, arrogant, negative person? Or just the opposite?
2. Attitudes are adjustable. Attitudes aren't fixed forever. Attitudes can adjust quickly, if you want them to change and are willing to work to change them. You're not doomed to a life of bad attitudes. Just be willing to make the improvements.
3. Accept responsibility for your attitudes. To keep good attitudes, own responsibility for them. We have to choose the right thoughts and responses to people who attack, irritate, frustrate, or agitate us, and to trials and tribulations we go through.
4. Appreciate and affirm. When others attempt to infect you with an ugly attitude, don't buy into the bad stuff. Affirm the good. Bless instead of curse. Be an ambassador of hope, love, joy, faith, unity and harmony, humility and peace. Don't get dragged into the cesspool others swim in. Keep your head up, and keep your heart up.
5. Ask for God's help. Demonstrating good attitudes consistently requires a source of strength. We need God's help, power, and grace.

Practice these five and you'll be amazed at the difference they will make. You'll be happier, and the people around you will be blessed.

Get Growing!

How do you manage your attitudes in ways that please God and benefit the people around you?

Wake Up!

And do this, understanding the present time. The hour has come for you to wake up from your slumber, because our salvation is nearer now than when we first believed. The night is nearly over; the day is almost here. So let us put aside the deeds of darkness and put on the armor of light.
Romans 13:11-12 (NIV)

When the sound of our alarm clock reaches our ears each morning, it's a declaration that a particular time has come. It's time to arise and prepare to fulfill the responsibilities that are scheduled for our day.

The Apostle Paul reminds us of the critical nature of the days in which we live. He gives us a three-point call to direct our thoughts, attitudes and actions every day.

First, we are called to "understand the present time." He describes the present time as an hour when "our salvation is nearer than when we first believed." In other words, the present time is the time when the Second Coming of Christ is approaching.

With this in mind, he gives us a second call. *"The hour has come for you to wake up from your slumber."* Because that day is rapidly approaching, we cannot afford to spend our days in spiritual slumber. It's time to rise from our sleep and decide to serve the Lord.

Third, if we are to effectively and seriously serve the Lord, we must be properly dressed for our responsibilities and challenges. He reminds us that we are to take off a certain set of clothes and put on another. We are to *"put aside the deeds of darkness and put on the armor of light."* We are to be prepared for "that day" by putting on the right clothing!

We are called to awaken to the reality that Christ is coming again. It's time to awaken. It's time to seriously consider the priorities of our lives. It's time to take off the *"deeds of darkness"* and be dressed in the *"armor of light."* It's time to prepare to win each battle against the influences of the world, our flesh, and the attacks of the devil.

Consider waking up *today* to God's alarm clock and be serious in serving God.

Get Growing!

- What deeds of darkness have you allowed in your life?
- What decisions will you make to eliminate them?

An Evangelistic Heart

Brothers, my heart's desire and prayer to God for the Israelites is that they may be saved. Romans 10:1 (NIV)

Perhaps one of the greatest needs in the church today is the need for people who possess an "evangelistic heart." Large segments of the church refer to themselves as "evangelical" believers.

Evangelicals believe in the importance of sharing the good news that salvation is available to all who are willing to place their faith and trust in Christ Jesus as the Savior and Lord of their lives. Unfortunately, many who carry the name "evangelical" have either lost, or never developed, a truly "evangelistic heart." What do we mean by this phrase, and what is involved in possessing or developing an "evangelistic heart?"

No one better exemplifies what I mean by this phrase than the Apostle Paul. You can see in the verse of Scripture above his all-consuming passion for the salvation of others. Although Paul was uniquely called as an apostle to the Gentiles, his heart also burned with a desire for the salvation of his fellow Israelites.

By observing Paul's life, we can learn several characteristics of an individual who possesses an evangelistic heart. Let's look at five of these characteristics.

A person with an evangelistic heart:

- understands both the temporal and eternal consequences experienced by those who are lost.
- feels and expresses God's compassion for people who have no personal relationship with Christ.

- is committed to "evangelistic intercession."
- understands the pathway that will lead a person to true salvation.
- is willing and equipped to communicate this pathway of salvation to others.

To develop an evangelistic heart, begin to ask God to give you a heart that loves and cares for people the way he does. Be willing to share your faith with others. See what Paul wrote: *"How, then, can they call on the one they have not believed in? And how can they believe in the one of whom they have not heard? And how can they hear without someone preaching to them? (or sharing with them)"* (Romans 10:14).

Let's choose to become people who possess "evangelistic hearts."

Get Growing!

- Do you possess an "evangelistic heart"? Are you living with a genuine concern for those around you who have yet to discover the wonderful truth of salvation?
- Who do you know that needs to hear about Jesus, from your neighbors, co-workers, relatives or acquaintances? Are you willing to lovingly and compassionately share your faith in Jesus Christ with them?

There Is Hope for You

There are three things that will endure—faith, hope, and love. 1 Corinthians 13:13 (NLT)

Please prepare a guest room for me, for I am hoping that God will answer your prayers and let me return to you soon. Philemon 1:22 (NLT)

Hope is one of the most powerful and positive resources we can possess, and one of the enduring, eternal qualities that we need as part of our lives. The Bible is big on hope. Hope involves having a positive dream and vision for our future. Hope involves looking ahead with the confidence and assurance that God has something good ahead for us. Hope enables us to envision and imagine God's best, so we will never settle for less.

The Apostle Paul was a man of great hope, which enabled him to see life differently. When Paul wrote this passage, he was incarcerated, walled in, his life under the control of others. Paul was physically restricted, but his hope was not. Through the power of hope, Paul reached beyond the confining walls into a future of freedom. Paul said, "I am hoping." These words describe an ongoing action—something Paul was doing and refused to quit doing!

Because hope is such an important quality in our lives, we can be sure that the devil works hard to quench, dilute, and rob us of hope. Many people have never developed hope, or their hope has been diminished or stolen.

One of the most telling signs of weakened or lost hope is the sense that change is not possible. People struggling with hopelessness are identified by some basic mindsets:

- "I can't change."
- "Others are never going to change."
- "My circumstances can't change."

We cannot change others, nor can we always change our circumstances, but it is inappropriate to say that people or circumstances *never* change. Both people and circumstances *can* and *do* change!

Hope-filled people have a different mindset, one controlled by positive thoughts that declare:

- "God can change people for good!"
- "God can change circumstances for good!"
- "God can change me for good!"

Hope is essential for spiritual, emotional and relational success. Hope starts when we start seeing life differently.

Get Growing!

- Has hopelessness robbed you from believing that God can change your circumstance?
- In what areas of your life are you hoping to see a change? What practical steps are you taking to see the change happen?

Spiritual Energy

Never be lacking in zeal, but keep your spiritual fervor, serving the Lord. Be joyful in hope, patient in affliction, faithful in prayer. Romans 12:11-12 (NIV)

Have you ever felt like your spiritual energy was depleted? I am sure we all have experienced times in our lives when we felt that our spiritual batteries were drained.

The Apostle Paul provides us with a clear admonition regarding the importance of maintaining our spiritual energy in the midst of the ever-present pressures of daily living. There are many potential obstacles facing us as Christian believers. Perhaps two of the most common obstacles are spiritual apathy and discouragement.

"Apathy" means "indifference, lack of interest or concern." "Spiritual apathy" involves the loss of spiritual concern. We grow cold in our relationship with God. We may continue to attend church, we may even maintain some level of communication with God, yet, internally, we have lost our enthusiasm for Christ and his kingdom. In the words of the Apostle Paul we *"lose our spiritual fervor and zeal."*

The other dangerous obstacle to a joyous Christian life is discouragement. The discouraged person is the one who has grown tired and weary from persistent pressures, unfulfilled goals and uncooperative circumstances. Discouragement is one of the most serious diseases of the soul. It depletes us internally, robbing our hope, casting shadows of doubt on our faith.

Today's passage instructs us to avoid both of these deadly traps. We must not lose our spiritual zeal and fervor. We are to maintain a patient hope during our times of difficulty. How do we fulfill these instructions? The Holy Spirit gives us an important key. We are to be *"faithful in prayer."* The believer who makes a commitment to faithfulness in prayer will find that their spirit is recharged, refueled, and refreshed. A consistent and disciplined prayer life is a pathway to streams of quiet waters where our spirit and soul are restored.

Perhaps you feel like your spiritual battery has lost some of its charge. Maybe you have been discouraged over certain events that have occurred in your life. Seek the renewal of the Lord. You can overcome apathy and discouragement. Commit to spend time with God daily and boost your spiritual energy.

Get Growing!

- How would you describe your spiritual energy? Do you feel an enthusiasm for God and his kingdom?
- How do you fight discouragement in your walk with God?
- What can you do to remain encouraged with increasing spiritual energy?

Friendship

Is there anyone still left of the house of Saul to whom I can show kindness for Jonathan's sake? 2 Samuel 9:1 (NIV)

It has been said that one good friend is more valuable than a thousand acquaintances. It's true that a real friend is a great blessing, and too often, a rarity.

What is friendship? Friendships are characterized by emotional connection and positive chemistry between people, yet they are much more than this. Real friendships are all about lifting, helping, encouraging, and challenging growth in one another. They are about care, commitment, endurance, and longevity. They are about selflessness. They are about deep bonds of loyalty and devotion.

One of the great stories of friendship in the Bible is that of David and his dear friend Jonathan. Jonathan was the son of Israel's first king, Saul. He was heir-apparent to his dad's throne. But Jonathan knew something that caused him to freely forfeit his right to succeed his father. He knew that a young man named David was God's pick to lead the nation.

Denying any natural inclination for pride or jealousy, and giving no thought to any personal ambitions, Jonathan graciously became David's friend and helper. He encouraged David in tough times. He protected him from destructive schemes. He pledged and demonstrated loyalty to David over and over again. Jonathan did everything he possibly could to help David reach his God-designed destiny as the king of Israel. What an amazing friend.

Although Jonathan's life ended on the battlefield, David never forgot him, and never stopped appreciating his friendship. Many years after Jonathan's death, David asked a question that revealed his enduring gratitude for his great friend. From this inquiry, David located Jonathan's son, Mephibosheth. Mephibosheth was poor, depressed and disabled, but David befriended him, took him in and took care of him for the rest of his life. He did this as a statement of his abiding appreciation for Jonathan.

The lesson? *Friendships impact people for a lifetime. You never forget a real friend.*

I'm sure we'd all like to have a friend like Jonathan. While we cannot create "Jonathans" in our lives, we can choose to be a Jonathan-like friend to someone. Go ahead and be a real friend to somebody. Start today!

Get Growing!

- What true friends are in your life?
- What steps can you take to invest in and nurture the wonderful relationships God has given to you?

Captive

Then a new king, to whom Joseph meant nothing, came to power in Egypt. "Look," he said to his people, "the Israelites have become far too numerous for us." ...So they put slave masters over them to oppress them with forced labor... They made their lives bitter with harsh labor in brick and mortar and with all kinds of work in the fields; in all their harsh labor the Egyptians worked them ruthlessly. Exodus 1:8-14 (NIV)

Have you ever felt as though you were living in captivity? The Book of Exodus addresses the issues of slavery, bondage, and the pathway to freedom. It opens with the Israelites living in slavery. They had come to Egypt through the leadership of Joseph and experienced many blessings, growing from a small extended family of approximately seventy people into a nation, two million strong. They were happy. They enjoyed abundance. They did not expect their condition to change, but they became enslaved.

We may have never experienced the pain of physical slavery, yet all of us know something about the slavery of being controlled by a dominating force or influence. Many people know about being enslaved to things, to actions, to attitudes, to destructive thoughts and lifestyles.

In Exodus, we find a picture of the common spiritual condition of all humanity. Every person is born into this world under the bondage of sin and under the authority of an evil ruler who desires to use us for his purposes, to the point of our own eternal destruction. Even as Christian believers, we often continue to live under the dominion of the evil king who conscripts us into slavery.

The need of the human soul and spirit is to find freedom from this bondage. We need to be delivered from the controlling forces that captivate us. We need to be emancipated and liberated. But, emancipation and liberation will not come until we take the first step toward freedom. The first step is being willing to acknowledge to yourself the reality of your bondage, and then acknowledge it to God and others. Bondages in our lives will never be broken as long as we ignore the reality of their existence. There is only one thing worse than slavery itself. That is, to be a slave and not even know it, or to deny it.

Allow the Lord to reveal any areas of bondage in your life today. As he reveals them, move toward freedom by openly admitting them to yourself, then to God, and as he leads, to others. As you do, you will begin to move down the pathway that leads to true freedom.

Get Growing!

- What areas of your life are under some type of bondage?
- What decisions do you need to make to experience the true freedom that God desires for your life?

Establishing a Reputation

I commend to you our sister Phoebe, a servant of the church in Cenchrea. I ask you to receive her in the Lord in a way worthy of the saints and to give her any help she may need from you, for she has been a great help to many people, including me. Romans 16:1-2 (NIV)

How is your reputation?

Every person is in the process of building this thing called "a reputation." A reputation is "the way people evaluate another person's character." It involves the way others view you, what they think about the integrity of your life.

A reputation is something that a person builds over a period of time. As we interact with people through the days, months, and years, our actions and attitudes build our reputation with them.

When the Apostle Paul comes to the conclusion of his epistle to the Roman believers, he expresses his love and appreciation to a number of individuals who had developed a positive reputation in his heart and mind. Their reputation had been established through certain attributes and actions that were genuinely evident in their lives.

The Apostle Paul encourages the believers in Rome to receive a lady named Phoebe. She was a part of the local church in Cenchrea, which was a port city of Corinth. Phoebe was most probably the one who was to deliver this letter to the church at Rome. The early church practiced a process of "letters of commendation." When one believer traveled to another locality, a letter of commendation from their home church was an important document for them to present when they found a new church fellowship. The letter of commendation was a declaration of the person's reputation among those who had observed the quality of their life.

Phoebe was a lady who possessed a great reputation. Her life had been observed by the Apostle Paul and he commended her for some important qualities. Note the three things that impressed the Apostle about this woman. First, she was a true servant of the church. Second, *she had been a great help to many people.* And third, she had been a great help to the Apostle Paul.

What kind of reputation are you building in your life? Choose to build a good reputation through your actions and attitudes starting today.

Get Growing!

- Can you name a person that you consider having a great reputation? What are the attributes of this person?
- How can you build the same attributes for your life?

Next Level of Faith

*And without faith it is impossible to please God,
because anyone who comes to him must believe that
he exists and that he rewards those who earnestly seek
him. Hebrews 11:6 (NIV)*

Faith connects us to God and to all the gifts and blessings
he wants to give us. Faith is one of the keys to a peaceful
and productive life. One of the best ways to grow faith is
by focusing on God's nature and character. When we realize
who he is, our faith goes to new levels. Use this acrostic to
remember some key qualities of God's nature and character
that will build and strengthen your faith. God is:

F = Faithful. To be faithful is to be reliable in character.
God can always be counted on to do what he says and
fulfill what he has promised. God is completely reliable.
He will never let you down.

A = Available and approachable. It is incredible to think
that the God of the universe, the Almighty Creator,
makes himself available to us. He invites us to approach
him with whatever problems, pains, needs, and concerns
we have.

I = Interested. God is available, approachable, and
interested. He pays close attention to us when we come
to Him. He is touched by the things we bring to Him.

T = Trustworthy. When we come to God with our needs,
we can trust that he knows what is best for us. He is a

God of integrity, love, grace, and mercy. He will never lead us astray or leave us alone. Even when we cannot see him at work or feel his presence, we can trust that he is with us, advancing his perfect plan for us.

H = Helpful. "*Helpful*" seems like a significant understatement in describing God. But far from minimal or moderate assistance, when it comes to God, the word takes on a whole new meaning. God is "*helpful.*" He is "*full of help.*" He intervenes, acts on our behalf, and empowers.

God is a Savior, Healer, Deliverer, Emancipator, Redeemer! All of these titles point to the powerful help God gives to people who look to him.

Get Growing!

- Take a look how the writer of Hebrews describes all of these qualities of God: *So then, since we have a great High Priest who has entered heaven, Jesus the Son of God, let us hold firmly to what we believe. This High Priest of ours understands our weaknesses, for he faced the same testings we do, yet he did not sin. So let us come boldly to the throne of our gracious God. There we will receive his mercy, and we will find grace to help us when we need it most (Hebrews 4:14-16 NLT).*
- How would you describe God?

When "It's" Gone

The wine supply ran out during the festivities.
John 2:3 (NLT)

We all have faced a situation when we ran short, or perhaps totally ran out of something we desperately needed. It could be limited financial resources to meet a pressing bill. It might be the loss of focus, inspiration, energy or motivation to get a job done. It could be the wearing down, or perhaps the complete erosion of love, passion and connection in a relationship. There are times in life when "it's" gone—whatever that "it" might be.

In the Gospel of John, a story is told about a time when some wedding hosts found themselves in such a situation. It the midst of a weeklong marriage celebration, the wine for the guests ran out. Although this might have been a bit upsetting, inconvenient, and embarrassing for the hosts, we would all agree that it is not exactly the worst catastrophe in the world. Nevertheless, it was a genuine problem. In this case the "it" was the reception refreshments, and "it" was gone!

Jesus, his mother, and family were at the celebration. After learning about the situation, Jesus' mother appealed to him to intervene and he did. Jesus requested that six large water jars be filled with water. Then he miraculously turned the water into wine. The problem was solved and the celebration resumed. According to those overseeing the festivities, things were better afterwards than they had been before.

There are lots of important lessons in this story for us. The basic one is very simple, but significant. Jesus cares about losses and limitations in our lives. When our "it" runs low or runs out, he is concerned, and he is willing to help. He stands ready to step in and restore what is lost when we ask him to do so. He is ready to intervene in our restricted or depleted situations, capabilities, relationships, and emotions. He will take the ordinary resources that we have and miraculously produce something extraordinary that we need. What he supplies is always more than sufficient. When we appeal to him, he creates something better than before.

Take your needs to Jesus. He is the One who turned water to wine at the wedding celebration in Cana over 2,000 years ago. He will do the same for you, too!

Get Growing!

- What is your "it" today? What is in short supply in your life?
- Take a moment to thank God for his timely and sufficient provision in the past and trust he will provide what you need today.

Taking Control of Your Thoughts

Be careful what you think, because your thoughts run your life. Proverbs 4:23 (NCV)

If anything is excellent or praiseworthy—think about such things. Philippians 4:8 (NIV)

Don't copy the behavior and customs of this world, but let God transform you into a new person by changing the way you think. Then you will learn to know God's will for you, which is good and pleasing and perfect. Romans 12:2 (NLT)

Casting down arguments and every high thing that exalts itself against the knowledge of God, bringing every thought into captivity to the obedience of Christ. 2 Corinthians 10:5 (NKJV)

The single most powerful part of your body is your mind. Our thinking affects everything we do. How we think determines our character, attitudes, and actions.

It should not surprise us that the devil targets our minds. This is his preferred place to attack. If our spiritual adversary can gain access to our thinking process, he can deceive us, distract us, and potentially destroy us.

Not all thoughts originate inside our own heads. Thoughts come to us from outside our own minds as well—through the things we watch and listen to, the conversations we have, and through the suggestions and lies of our invisible but very real spiritual adversary.

Here is an important truth to remember: Until we learn to set up a defense system around our minds, the devil will consistently and persistently ransack and ravage us with deceptive, distracting, and destructive thoughts. How do we put up a defense system around our minds?

When we "hear" a thought knocking at the door of our mind, we need to inspect it before we let it in. If it is an unworthy thought, we need to reject it as an adversarial force trying to invade us. We must refuse to let it into our minds, much like we would refuse a suspicious stranger from stepping into our house.

Success or failure, victory or defeat first happens in the head! Change your life by changing your thinking.

Get Growing!

- What areas of your life have been damaged by ungodly and negative thoughts?
- Join me in this prayer: *"Dear Lord, help me to discern ungodly and negative thoughts and establish a spiritual defense system against them. May all deceptive, distracting and destructive thoughts I have allowed into our minds be driven from me now. Help me to reject every thought that draws me away from your Word and will. In Jesus' Name, Amen."*

Improve Your Serve

Jesus knew that the Father had put him in complete charge of everything, that he came from God and was on his way back to God. So he got up from the supper table, set aside his robe, and put on an apron. Then he poured water into a basin and began to wash the feet of the disciples, drying them with his apron. John 13:3-5 (MSG)

Service is a big deal. Restaurants, hotels, companies, and corporations are sometimes judged more by their service than by their products. Wise leaders work hard at "improving the serve" of their organization. Why? Because pleasant, responsive, thorough, and gracious service is a key to building something great.

According to Jesus, service is one of the keys to building a great life. In the passage above, you can see that Jesus didn't just teach about serving, he lived it.

This is one of the most moving stories of the New Testament. In it, we see Jesus' example of unexpected, amazing service. The story takes place the night before Jesus' crucifixion. Jesus assembles his disciples in a room in Jerusalem for a meal, the "Last Supper."

As the disciples gather that evening, an important act of service is ignored. It was the custom at times like this for the dusty and muddy feet of dinner guests to be washed when they arrived at the host's home. Foot washing was a lowly job, usually performed by a servant in the house, or by the host of the meal as a statement of care, kindness, and hospitality. It was a way to show love to the people present.

None of the disciples volunteered for this task. They all felt too important to be washing their fellow disciples' feet. They wanted dignity, prestige, greatness. In fact, part of the conversation that evening included a contentious debate among the disciples about which one of them was the greatest (Luke 22:24).

How many times do we think and act the same way Jesus' disciples did? Our attitude is "I don't do feet! I'm too important for such menial tasks!"

Part of becoming a true follower of Jesus includes letting go of the pride and sense of self-importance that keep us from developing a servant's heart. Jesus washed the disciples' feet. If Jesus can wash feet, so can we, and so should we.

While literal foot washing is not something needed in our culture today, there are many other ways we can provide acts of humble service to others. It's time for all of us to "improve our serve."

Get Growing!

- In what ways, have you ignored or "thought too much of yourself" to serve others?
- What can you start doing today to improve your serve?

The Power of a Song

About midnight Paul and Silas were praying and singing hymns to God.... Suddenly, there was such a violent earthquake that the foundations of the prison were shaken. At once all the prison doors flew open, and everybody's chains came loose. Acts 16:25-26 (NIV)

You are my hiding place; you will protect me from trouble and surround me with songs of deliverance. Psalm 32:7 (NIV)

Throughout history, churches have been and continue to be places of music and song. Many of the greatest and grandest musical compositions ever penned have been inspired by faith and written for the glory of God. Over the centuries, churches have been known for their choirs and organs, and in more contemporary times, for their worship teams. Why? Why is music such an integral part of church life?

There are many reasons why music has a key role in the life of Christian believers. It is a powerful way to communicate praise to the God who created us and the Son of God, Jesus, who saved us through his death and resurrection. To raise our voice in songs of praise to magnify, honor, and glorify God is something every Christian longs to do.

I have been thinking about the power of song in a more personal way. I was reminded of a couple of passages in the Bible that emphasize the life-shaping and devil-defeating impact of singing songs of worship and praise.

Paul and Silas were set free from their literal prison because of their commitment to prayer and singing God's praise. Their deliverance came as a direct result of them being willing to lift up a song in a tough place, in a difficult set of circumstances. The result was a powerful deliverance. The psalmist reminded us of the same truth—songs of worship, lifted in faith, have power to deliver.

Whatever tough situation you are facing or darkness you are battling, let me encourage you to do what Paul and Silas did. Begin lifting up songs of praise to God and expect breakthroughs to come! Sing! Sing! Sing!

Get Growing!

- Has there been a time when you experienced the power of a song?
- What can you do to develop a life of praising and worshipping the Lord? Make the decision to lift up songs of praise to God in every circumstance of your life!

After the Fall

When the woman saw that the fruit of the tree was good for food and pleasing to the eye, and also desirable for gaining wisdom, she took some and ate it. She also gave some to her husband, who was with her, and he ate it.
Genesis 3:6 (NIV)

Whether we recognize it or not, all of us have been subjected to a devastating fall. Going back to the Garden of Eden, we find Adam and Eve yielding to the temptation propagated by the serpent. As they succumbed to this temptation, the Bible clearly teaches us that Adam and Eve experienced a destructive fall. Spiritually, emotionally, and even physically, humanity fell into the bondage and slavery of sin. The taskmaster of sin is cruel and ruthless, and its presence in our lives exacts a significant cost.

The good news is this. Although we were born under the curse of this captivity, severely damaged by the fall into sin, God has graciously intervened. The story of the Bible from Genesis to Revelation is the story of redemption. It's the story of liberation. This sums it up well: *"For God so loved the world that he gave his one and only Son, that whoever believes in him shall not perish but have eternal life"* (John 3:16). This passage promises to us a way out of captivity, a pathway that will free us from sin's bondage.

Many people can testify to Christ's liberating power. By a simply act of repentance and faith in the death and resurrection of Christ, our freedom is secured. Yet we must also understand that following our liberation, Christ has purposed to bring us through a process of restoration. Years of living in sin's bondage leave a mark on us. There are broken pieces in our lives that must be put back together. There are bruised points that desperately need to be healed. Christ not only cares about our liberation, he also cares about our restoration.

Christ has provided resources to us, which will lead us through this process of restoration. He has given us the Holy Spirit. The Holy Spirit works in our lives revealing the broken points, pouring in the healing oil, restoring in us a confident assurance of the Heavenly Father's love. The Holy Spirit also leads us into God's truth that begins to clean out the hidden places and renews our minds so that we can think right and righteous thoughts.

Just as liberation from sin requires our cooperation with God's redemptive plan, so does restoration from sin.

Christ has come, not only as our liberator, but also as our restorer. Let's open our hearts and allow him to begin putting the broken places of our lives together, today.

Get Growing!

- In what areas of your life do you need Jesus as a liberator?
- In what areas of your life do you need Jesus to be a restorer?

How to Have a Good Day

The faithful love of the Lord never ends! His mercies never cease. Great is his faithfulness; his mercies begin afresh each morning. Lamentations 3:22-23 (NLT)

"Have a good day!" It's a nice thing to hear and say. Obviously wishing someone a "good day" is better than the alternative—wishing them a "bad day!" But what is a "good day," and how do we know if we're having one?

Most often we think of a good day as one that goes well—a day when good things come our way. It's a day absent of bad news, bad feelings, bad interactions, bad attitudes, and bad behavior. We think of it as a day when the right things happen to us, and the wrong things do not. The downside to this description is that it is entirely at the mercy of outside forces—other people, outside circumstances and uncontrollable events. When all these are positive, we are good, and when they are not—what?

An important step on the path to maturity is learning to live from the inside out rather than from the outside in. It's learning to be a "thermostat" rather than a "thermometer." The first sets the environment, the second displays the conditions with no influence. A "thermometer" reflects what is. A "thermostat" determines what will be.

What does this mean for "having a good day?" Life changes for the better when we realize that the quality of our day can be determined by us. We're not at the mercy of outside forces for happiness. We can set the environment of a day by our choices and attitudes. We can think and act in ways that create a "good day" instead of hoping or wishing a good day would "happen" to us.

To set yourself up for a good day, everyday, try this:

- Turn worries into prayers. Give your cares and concerns to God each day.
- Be grateful. Express appreciation to God and others for the good things you have been given.
- Pray for others. Think about people who are facing tough stuff. Take their needs to God in prayer.
- Practice kindness, grace and generosity. Purposely plan to be kind. Be a forgiver. Give something to someone everyday.
- Read your Bible and reflect on it. If it's only for a short time each day, get into God's Word and let God's Word get into you!
- Turn the events of your day into life lessons. Become a student. Learn everything you can from life.
- Practice praise. Praise God for who he is, for what he has done for you, for what he's doing for you, and for what he's going to do in and through your life. And be generous with your praise of others to get rid of selfish and self-centered thinking.

Get Growing!

Set a goal to write down ten blessings a day for the next seven days. You will realize how "good" your days are!

Peace

Peace I leave with you; my peace I give you. I do not give to you as the world gives. Do not let your hearts be troubled and do not be afraid. John 14:27 (NIV)

How much peace do you possess in your life? One of the things we all search for and seek after is peace. Peace can be defined in a number of ways. It's a word that is used to describe "a state of tranquility or quietness." It's also used to describe "harmony in particular relationships." Peace is something that all of us desire in our personal lives, as well as in our interpersonal interactions with others.

One of the greatest hindrances to peace, personally and interpersonally, is something called stress. The Christian psychologist, Archibald Hart, states in one of his books that "the time is rapidly approaching, if it hasn't already arrived, when we will be dying less and less from infectious disease but more and more from the ravaging effects of too much stress."

Stress can be defined as "pressure that is exerted upon our lives physically, spiritually and psychologically." It has been said that stress can result from anything that: annoys you, threatens you, prods you, excites you, scares you, worries you, hurries you, angers you, frustrates you, challenges you, or criticizes you. As you can see from this list, not everything that might cause stress is necessarily negative. In fact, stress can actually result in positive growth in our lives. The issue is not whether we will experience stress. We will. The critical factor is how we respond to it when it arrives.

In today's passage, Christ speaks to his disciples during a time of great stress in their lives. After walking with Christ for three years, they suddenly found themselves facing the reality that he was soon going to depart from them. The thought of this was too much for them to bear. Christ knew that this was both a difficult and challenging time for his disciples, a time that called them to new growth. Growing through this stress required supernatural peace.

In these words, Christ promises something to his disciples, a resource that would carry them through their time of stress. It was his peace—a peace that would overcome the fear and turmoil in their hearts.

Perhaps you are facing some stress in your life. Reach out and receive the peace that passes all understanding. Receive the peace of God in your life today!

Get Growing!

- What are the greatest internal and external stress factors in your life?
- What lessons have you learned from stressful situations?
- What steps can you take to allow Christ into stressful moments of your daily life?
- How can you help others around you to live a less stressful life?

Avoiding Viruses

*Don't hang out with angry people; don't keep company
with hotheads. Bad temper is contagious—don't get
infected.* Proverbs 22:24-25 (MSG)

*Do not be deceived: "Bad company corrupts good
morals." 1 Corinthians 15:33 (NAS)*

Have you ever been in a confined place with someone
who was coughing or sneezing without concern about
others around them? This happens frequently in
elevators, waiting rooms, lobbies, offices, airplanes,
and in other environments.

If you are like me, you want to distance yourself from
the germs that are being projected into your world. While
you may have compassion on the suffering person, you do
not want to catch whatever it is that they have. You go into
protective mode. You may politely and carefully withdraw
a bit from the person. You probably hold your breath for a
moment or two and remove yourself from the environment
as soon as possible.

The same wisdom can be applied to another area of life.
As surely as physical viruses can be caught from others, bad
attitudes can be caught too. The Bible teaches us that bad
attitudes are contagious. Here's some good steps to take
the next time you are around someone who is "coughing
and sneezing" bad attitudes—negativity, gossip, anger, fear,
worry, and any other spiritual or emotional virus:

- Recognize it. Be alert to potential spiritual and
  emotional germs around you.

- Respond to it. If you have a relationship with the person, give them some feedback about what you are seeing or hearing from them.
- Refuse to receive it. Make a conscious decision that you are not going to be infected by the person.
- Remove yourself from the situation. Get away from an infected person or environment as soon as you can.
- Refresh right attitudes after the exposure. After removing yourself, recheck and refresh attitudes in your heart. Make sure no viral residue remains in you.

Do not let someone else's spiritual and emotional germs get into your system. Avoid infection!

Get Growing!

- Who are the people surrounding you that often "cough and sneeze" a bad attitude?
- What proactive steps can you take to avoid getting contaminated by others' attitudes?

Genuine Worshipers

You shall not make for yourself an image in the form of anything in heaven above or on the earth beneath or in the waters below. You shall not bow down to them or worship them; for I, the Lord your God, am a jealous God. Exodus 20:4-5 (NIV)

Perhaps one of the most sobering moments in Cecil B. DeMille's motion picture "The Ten Commandments" is the time when Moses goes to the top of Mount Sinai to receive the commandments from God. In the movie, as God had just inscribed the second commandment upon the tablet of stone, "You shall not make yourself a graven image," the camera shifts to the foot of the mountain where the Israelites were singing and dancing around the golden calf. This dramatically portrays for us the need for this second commandment.

In the passage above, God gives the definition and direction for our worship of him. This second commandment is a call from God for us to become single-hearted, genuine worshipers of him and him only. A healthy life involves learning and choosing to worship God in the right way. This commandment declares that we must not *"make God in our image."* In other words, our worship of God must be free from all false images of him.

The second commandment teaches us that healthy worship involves possessing a right and healthy image of God. Any man-made image of God is inadequate and insufficient to describe the beauty and majesty of his nature. Perhaps the most subtle and dangerous violation of this commandment has to do with false internal images of God.

We may have a distorted image of what God really is like. These wrong images are dangerous and destructive to us spiritually and emotionally because they affect and control our trust or confidence in God. This certainly affects our worship of him. We will never be a genuine worshiper of God until we begin to develop a true picture of the real nature of God!

God forbids us from making an image of him because he himself provided his own image in his son Christ Jesus! *"He (Jesus) is the image of the invisible God, the firstborn over all creation"* (Colossians 1:15).

Are you a "genuine worshiper" of God? Remember that genuine worship flows from a genuine understanding of the nature of God. Put in your heart a fresh revelation of his nature today!

Get Growing!

What does the God on the throne of your heart look like? Have you formed your concept of him based upon your own life experiences or have you formed your image of God based upon the revelation of Jesus Christ?

It's Good to Give Thanks — Part 1

I will give thanks to the Lord. Psalm 7:17 (NIV)

We often need to be reminded of something that should be deeply ingrained in our character—gratitude. The Bible is full of exhortations to give thanks, both to God and to people, for the blessings and gifts given to us. Gratitude, or the lack of it, says a lot about us. Grateful people have a quality that blesses God and others, and serves them well, too. An attitude of gratitude brings great benefits to us. Look at what gratitude does for us:

1. Gratitude changes our perspective. Perspective is the lens through which we view our world. We can easily allow our perspective on life to be skewed, tainted, darkened, soured, and consumed by our personal struggles and stresses. We tend to highlight the lacks and losses in our lives. Gratitude demands something from us. It pushes us to look past our lack and losses to see gifts and gains. Gratitude forces us to focus on the good, to adjust the lens of our perspective to a more realistic view—a view that includes the incredible blessings we have received that are not always obvious. With an adjustment of perspective comes a fresh joy, a new hope, an awareness that, notwithstanding whatever struggles and stresses may be a part of our lives, the truth is, we're blessed.

2. Gratitude helps confront and conquer worry and fear. Worry and fear are two of life's biggest bullies. These two attackers shackle, chain, and imprison people. They paralyze us from productive actions and blind us to

potential opportunities. One of the most repeated commands given by God in Scripture is: "Don't be afraid!" Or, "Fear not!"

In the Old Testament, God instructed his people to build memorials to remind them of God's awesome power and love, and of the great miracles he had performed for them. Gazing on these memorials was to be more than a happy stroll down memory lane. The memorials were designed to give God's people faith and hope in facing current trials. They were meant to be a reminder of God's continual watchful care and readiness to help—a reminder to give people comfort, courage, and peace for the present, as they expressed their gratitude to God for his past work. They were to give people strength and assurance.

How do we combat worry and fear? Some would say, "through faith and trust," which is correct. But I offer you another weapon, another Bible method to fight fear and worry—*gratitude!*

Get Growing!

Take time to reflect about all the great things God has done in your life. After that, make a list of the small and big things you are thankful for.

It's Good to Give Thanks — Part 2

I will give thanks to the Lord. Psalm 7:17 (NIV)

The Bible is full of exhortations to give thanks—to God and to people. What does gratitude do for us?

1. Gratitude grows grace. One of the greatest qualities a person can possess is graciousness. People who are gracious are a pleasure to be around. They see the best, and work to bring out the best in others. To be called *"gracious"* is one of the highest expressions of praise that can be given.

   Gratitude makes us more gracious by focusing our attention on the graciousness of God and others. To be grateful, you must think about all the wonderful things God has done for you, the grace he has shown you, and the gracious things others have done for you.

   Your awareness of the grace of God and the graciousness of others inspires you to be and do the same. It encourages you to become a bigger, better, more gracious person. It provides you with an example to emulate. When you think about how good God has been to you, and how good others have been to you, you become more motivated to model the same attitudes and actions with others. Gratitude lifts you to higher places of grace and graciousness.

2. Gratitude confronts and curtails pride. Self-focused and self-centered pride is ugly, destructive, and severely condemned by God. God resists the proud. To get rid of this horrible enemy, embrace *gratitude*.

Real gratitude requires the acknowledgment and appreciation of what others have done for you. Gratitude, by its very nature, calls you to get your eyes off yourself and forces you to think about the contributions others have made in your life. Gratitude reminds you that your view of life and the world is better because someone has offered their shoulders for you to stand on. You experience blessings because others have made blessings possible.

3. Gratitude improves and strengthens the quality of relationships. More relationships die of neglect than abuse. We all tend to take people for granted, generally by not noticing the value and blessing they bring to us, or by failing to express our gratitude to them.

Remembering to say "thank you" keeps us focused on the value people add. Saying it makes us appreciate them more. Expressing appreciation to others is powerful.

Gratitude is beneficial, not only to others, but to us. Gratitude makes us better people. Gratitude gives us a better life. It's good to give thanks!

Get Growing!

Is thanksgiving a habit in your home? How can you engage yourself and your family in this new habit?

Leaders

If God has given you leadership ability, take the responsibility seriously. Romans 12:8 (NLT)

Good leadership is something that is needed in every part of our culture. In the home, church and community, God is looking for leaders—someone he can count on and use to positively influence people. What does it take? Here are a few ways to be a good leader:

1. Good leaders remember that someone is watching and taking their lead from them. They understand the importance of their example and influence. They conduct their lives with others in mind. They realize that real and positive leadership starts with being the right personal example to others.

2. Good leaders understand that responsibility is a good thing—something to be embraced, not avoided. Leadership is about accepting responsibility to be a servant, a help and blessing to others. It involves consistently choosing to demonstrate responsible actions and attitudes in all relationships and duties.

3. Good leaders are learning and growing. They have developed an appropriate degree of self-awareness that makes them sensitive to inconsistencies in their character and weaknesses in their example. As they see these things, they take action to address them. They have a teachable spirit.

4. Good leaders look back from time to time to carefully inspect the fruitfulness of those who are following them. Are good things happening in the lives of those they are influencing? Are they actually taking people under their care to new levels of spiritual life, character, productivity and responsibility? Are they growing? If not, they assess and determine what needs to be done to improve this situation. They take immediate, strategic steps to improve the quality of fruit they are producing.

5. Good leaders own up to their mistakes and failures. Nothing engenders respect more than an appropriate, honest, and sincere owning of one's mistakes and failures. Admitting to imperfections, weaknesses, and needed areas of growth helps followers do the same. It's an expression of humility that attracts God's grace in a person's life.

6. Good leaders are good followers. To be a good leader a person must first learn how to follow and how to maintain the characteristics of a good follower.

God is ready to help us become good leaders!

Get Growing!

- After reading some qualities of a good leader, how can you improve your leadership skills?
- Can you name a leader that you admire? What qualities do you admire most in that person?

Pause

Very early in the morning, while it was still dark, Jesus got up, left the house and went off to a solitary place, where he prayed. Mark 1:35 (NIV)

A couple of months ago my wife shared with me the essence of an article she had recently read in a Christian publication. It was titled "Pause." The basic theme was the importance of working strategic "pause moments" into life for the sake of reflection, renewal and recreation. The premise is that effectiveness in life and ministry is determined not just by the things we do, but also by taking time to "not do," by establishing strategic "pause moments" in our daily schedule.

In the passage above, we see that Jesus, during his earthly ministry, understood the value of the pause. It seems that Jesus started each day in "pause" mode. Before he launched into daily activities and responsibilities of ministry, Jesus found a solitary, quiet place to be alone with his Father. Everything he did during his days flowed out of the perspective and power he received from God during these vital times of pausing from the tasks and demands of hurting and lost people. This was a key to Jesus' ministry effectiveness.

Going back to Old Testament times, especially in the life of King David, we see the "pause principle" in operation. Whenever David took up his pen and poured his heart out to God on parchment, he would often land on "pause moments." Before he went any farther expressing himself in worship, prayer, or praise, we often observe him taking a moment to think about his words, his emotions and the greatness of his God.

During those times of reflection, David would insert a word into his poetry that let everyone know what he was doing. The word is "Selah." Roughly translated it means "to pause and think." "Selah" described David's commitment to take time out to reflect on God's greatness and power, and it's a command to all of us to do the same.

What about you? Are "pause moments" a part of your life?

Get Growing!

- Take a moment to examine how much of your day is dedicated to "pause" and prepare for the next task or activity. Is this a consistent thing in your life?
- What steps can you take to learn to "pause" and receive the benefits of an effective life and ministry?

Choose to Stretch

For when your faith is tested, your endurance has a chance to grow. So let it grow, for when your endurance is fully developed, you will be strong in character and ready for anything. James 1:3-4 (NLT)

The more you grow like this, the more you will become productive and useful in your knowledge of our Lord Jesus Christ. 2 Peter 1:8 (NLT)

God is *pro-growth*. All through Scripture, God consistently challenges people to take steps of growth and development. Personal growth is critical to fulfilling God's purpose and our potential.

If we go through life never increasing our capacity to handle challenges and responsibilities—or even shrinking in our capacity to handle them—we miss a significant portion of God's purpose for our lives. Growth is important to God!

What is essential for growth? What is required for growth? *Stress!* Some stress, in the form of challenges, obstacles, weights, responsibilities, and assignments, is necessary for growth to happen. Stress can be very good for us, if we respond the right way to it. Responding the right way to stress requires a change in attitude and perspective. We must learn to embrace growth opportunities that come with our stressful life experiences, assignments, and events.

Our tendency is to follow the path of least resistance—the easiest paths of life. By nature, we choose to avoid challenges. We love comfort. We pursue pleasure. We seek to avoid pain.

While we should not become gluttons for punishment and pain, there is a lot to be said for people who choose activities and responsibilities that stretch them beyond their comfort zone. How do we stretch?

- Challenge our self-imposed spiritual, mental and physical limitations.
- Do something that pushes us beyond our comfort zone.
- Pray for stretching.

When we pray for stretching, we can expect God to answer. Jabez discovered this. *Jabez was more honorable than his brothers. His mother had named him Jabez, saying, "I gave birth to him in pain." Jabez cried out to the God of Israel, "Oh, that You would bless me and enlarge my territory! Let Your hand be with me, and keep me from harm so that I will be free from pain." And God granted his request* (1 Chronicles 4:9-10 NIV).

Choose to stretch! You will be glad you did.

Get Growing!

- How is God stretching you? How are you responding to his prompting?
- In what areas of your life do you need to begin to allow God to stretch you more?

Extraordinary in the Ordinary

So beginning with this same Scripture, Philip told him the Good News about Jesus. Acts 8:35 (NLT)

It's been said that one of the challenging things about life is that it is so daily. Life is not always exciting, thrilling, or full of emotional highs and great feelings. Most of the time, life is very ordinary. We get up, get ready, go to work, do our job, come home, go to bed, and then do the same all over again the next day. We go through the routines of daily living. Nothing seems too special. It's just life!

In the flow of daily life, we often lose the expectation and anticipation of special moments. We fall into the rut of the ordinary and fail to look for the extraordinary. The ordinary anesthetizes us to the extraordinary. Because of this, we miss special moments and unique opportunities God brings our way.

In the Bible, God often showed up in unique and special ways in the lives of ordinary people doing ordinary things. The passage above is an example. Philip was a servant in the early church who loved to share his faith with others. One day, Philip was walking down a road and as he walked, God was talking to him.

Philip saw a chariot heading down the same road. The chariot happened to be transporting a very important official from Ethiopia. The Holy Spirit spoke to Philip and told him to go and walk alongside this carriage. Philip obeyed. When Philip approached the chariot, he heard this man reading from the scroll of Isaiah the prophet. Philip saw an extraordinary opportunity in an ordinary day.

Philip asked the official if he understood what he was reading. The man said that he needed some help. Philip offered his assistance, jumped in the chariot with him, and began telling the man about Jesus. This man accepted Christ that day and was baptized! A great moment in Philip's life happened because Philip looked for extraordinary, special moments in the midst of an ordinary day, doing an ordinary activity.

Yes, life is very daily and very ordinary. But remember, God has extraordinary, special moments and opportunities for you during your ordinary life and activities. Keep your spiritual eyes open to see them and your spiritual ears tuned to hear God's Spirit guiding you to embrace the unique, divine appointments in your daily life.

Get Growing!

- How sensitive are you to the voice of the Holy Spirit pointing you to divine appointments?
- What can you start doing today to become more aware of the "extraordinary" moments that God presents you in your daily living?

Faith or Feelings?

We live by faith, not by sight. 2 Corinthians 5:7 (NIV)

One of the most important lessons we can learn in our spiritual journey is to live by faith and not by our feelings. This is something many folks have a hard time understanding and putting into practice. Faith over feelings is a critical Kingdom principle.

The focus of our culture is very different. We are constantly bombarded with the message that feelings are like "god" to us. The world tells us that when emotions speak, we are obligated to act. The result is unnecessary problems and pain. When feelings are in charge, we will always make bad decisions.

Living by faith is a countercultural and counter-intuitive way to live. It means that we do what God asks us to do, whether we feel like doing it or not. It involves trusting that our obedience to God's Word—even when that obedience doesn't come with good feelings—it will bring blessings and positive results. Conducting ourselves according to this principle is essential to a solid and stable Christian walk and key to being used by God.

I think about all the prayers I would have never prayed, sermons I would have never preached, key decisions I would have never made, people I would have never met, if I had waited until I was "feeling" like it. I also think about the incredible things God has done in my life as a result of choosing to walk by faith and obedience instead of waiting for my emotions to inspire me to act.

Many years ago, I saw a little diagram in a booklet that really brought this truth home to me. It was a picture of a train—an engine, a railcar and a caboose. The engine was labeled "Faith," the railcar labeled "Obedience," and the caboose was labeled "Feelings."

The lesson of the diagram was clear. The power of the Christian life is found in the engine called faith. Linked to faith is obedience—doing what God says to do. Often the last thing to come along for the ride is our feelings. When we follow our feelings rather than our faith we put the caboose at the front of the train, and the result is no spiritual power or progress.

What comes first in your walk with the Lord, the engine, the railcar, or the caboose?

Get Growing!

- How are the messages of the world bombarding your faith in God?
- Have you ever made a decision based on feelings? What consequences did you have?

Finishing Strong

*In all my prayers for all of you, I always pray with joy
because of your partnership in the gospel from the first
day until now, being confident of this, that he who began
a good work in you will carry it on to completion until the
day of Christ Jesus. Philippians 1:4-6 (NIV)*

Have you ever started a project that you didn't complete?
Starting something is always much easier than finishing it.
Even when we begin a task or project with enthusiasm and
excitement, commitment and persistence are required to
take that project to the end.

We as human beings often fall short in these areas and
don't complete everything we begin, but there is One who
never fails in his commitment and persistence. Even a brief
study of the Bible reveals to us the portrait of God, our
heavenly Father, as One who begins good things and also
completes them.

Today's passage is a reminder of God's commitment to
complete every good work that he begins. Paul declared to
the believers in the city of Philippi that there was something
he was absolutely confident about concerning them. Not
only was *he* confident, he also wanted those *believers* to be
confident as well. The Amplified Bible interprets it, *"And I
am convinced and sure of this very thing."* What did Paul
want these believers to be convinced and sure of? That the
One who had begun a good work in their lives wasn't going
to leave the project partially completed. When Christ began
a good work in transforming their lives from darkness to
light, from sin to righteousness, from pain to peace, he
also committed himself to persistently work until the job

was done. All he asked of them was their obedience and cooperation.

We often look at our lives and see what seems to be a big mess—walls that need to be rebuilt, foundations that need to be laid, and holes that need to be mended. In our desperation, we wonder if the project will ever be completed.

The Lord desires to deposit within us a deep, abiding confidence that he never gives up on us, no matter how "messy" the project may be. He persistently works with us because he's committed to us. He has promised to carry on his good work in us until that work is completed. Allow the Holy Spirit to deposit within you a deep abiding confidence regarding the Lord's commitment to *you*.

Get Growing!

- How confident are you of the promises of God to your life? Do you know what they are?
- How can you increase your confidence in God?

Getting Hope

There are three things that will last forever—faith, hope, and love—and the greatest of these is love.
1 Corinthians 13:13 (NLT)

How much hope do you have? Hope is in short supply in our society. It doesn't take too many conversations with people to discover that depression, despondency, and despair are the order of the day.

It's hard to keep going without hope. Without hope, we wither internally. Without hope, we struggle to stay motivated. Without hope, many people give in to the problems and pressures of life—they simply give up the fight. Much self-destructive behavior in our world is the result of hopelessness. When hope levels run low, we live troubled lives and continue in troubled relationships. Hopeless people are sucked into the dark cells of cynicism, sarcasm, and sustained sadness.

The Apostle Paul identified three of the most important qualities in life: faith, hope, and love. It's interesting that he positioned hope in the center. It's impossible to have faith without first having hope. It's impossible to really love others, long-term, without hope. Hope is a kind of spiritual and emotional glue that holds life together.

Hope is not natural to human beings. Hope is a heavenly quality. The Bible teaches us that God is the source of hope. Strong, enduring hope comes through a relationship with him. When we open our hearts to Jesus Christ, we have the privilege of getting to know the God of hope. As we continue to learn more about him and live by the principles he has prescribed, our hearts our filled with a positive anticipation about our future. He gives us confidence about the good that lies ahead. He fills us with supernatural hope that enables us to see life differently—to see life from his perspective.

How can we tap into this supply of heavenly hope? We can start by focusing on God's goodness. When we realize how good God is, and understand that his goodness is personally directed to *us,* hope starts happening. When we begin believing that he has a wonderful, personalized plan for us, uniquely designed by him to fulfill all the potential he has placed in us, hope grows. We are filled with an awareness that our best is not behind us—it is in front of us!

Has your hope been running low? Know that God has a fresh supply of heavenly hope for you. Your best is yet to come.

Get Growing!

- Ask God to help you discover the steps you need to take to build hope in your life.
- Search and memorize several key Scripture verses that provide a hope promise for your future.

Good Advice When You Are Angry

A gentle answer deflects anger, but harsh words make tempers flare. Proverbs 15:1 (NLT)

Love prospers when a fault is forgiven, but dwelling on it separates close friends. Proverbs 17:9 (NLT)

A wise man restrains his anger and overlooks insults. Proverbs 19:11 (TLB)

Fools vent their anger, but the wise quietly hold it back. Proverbs 29:11 (NLT)

If you are angry, don't sin by nursing your grudge. Don't let the sun go down with you still angry—get over it quickly; for when you are angry, you give a mighty foothold to the devil. Ephesians 4:26-27 (TLB)

Stop being mean, bad- tempered, and angry. Quarreling, harsh words, and dislike of others should have no place in your lives. Instead, be kind to each other, tenderhearted, forgiving one another, just as God has forgiven you because you belong to Christ. Ephesians 4:31-32 (TLB)

Anger is a common human emotion—something we all experience. In and of itself, anger is not wrong or sinful, but it's dangerous. The words "anger" and "danger" are only one letter apart, which just serves to illustrate that anger gets you close to danger!

We live in an angry culture. People seething, stewing, and spewing are all around us. Anger rules some people and leaves behind a wake of pain and a host of casualties. When you are angry, you often say what you shouldn't say, behave in ways you shouldn't behave, and fight battles you shouldn't fight.

Angry attitudes and actions mess up marriages, ruin friendships, drain our emotional energy, cloud our judgment, reduce our productivity, prompt bad decisions, and even weaken our immunity. Medical researchers have discovered that hostility is horrible for your health—physically and psychologically. Anger and hostility are also some main causes for spiritual problems.

It's not just the "big anger" that gets us into trouble. Even small amounts of anger are dangerous, because whatever you focus on gets magnified in your mind and emotions. Given the right environment, small anger grows into big anger. The more you think and talk about how badly you feel someone treated you, how unfair some situation was, how rude a person behaved, how irritating or inconsiderate an individual is, the bigger the anger becomes in you. It is called "nursing your anger." And anything you nurse, grows.

Take your anger to God and allow him to restore your heart. God will heal you and help you toward an anger-free heart!

Get Growing!

- Think of a time when you let anger control you. What consequences did you experience?
- Are you angre at someone or something? What would you do differently this time?

Handling Disappointments

Yet you are enthroned as the Holy One; you are the one Israel praises. In you our ancestors put their trust; they trusted and you delivered them. To you they cried out and were saved; in you they trusted and were not put to shame.
Psalm 22:3-5 (NIV)

How do you handle disappointments? Everyone faces times of disappointment. The word "disappoint" means "to fail to meet the expectation or hope of something." When our expectations and dreams are not realized or fulfilled, we begin to feel a loss of motivation, a growing sense of anger, and a loss of hope for the future. For some people, a new disappointment is added to an accumulation of past disappointments. The result is cynicism and sometimes even despair.

What can we do when we are disappointed by life situations or by people? How do we respond and recover from these points in our lives?

1. To work our way through disappointments, it is vitally important to remember the beauty of God's personal love for us. When everything else seems to have failed, we must remember that his love never fails.
2. We must resolve and release our frustration, anger, and despair. This usually involves communication. We must talk out our disappointments with God and with other mature believers. The goal of this communication is resolution and release. Prayer is an extremely effective way to bring perspective to our disappointments.

3. We must rest in God's plan. God has a plan for our lives. When we resolve and release our negative emotions, we can recognize and rest in God's plan. He will work everything out for the good of those who love him and obey his word.
4. We must reestablish our trust in the Lord. Disappointments can erode trust. Finding victory over our disappointments involves the reestablishment of that trust.

Are you facing a disappointment in your life? Because of God's love, choose to resolve and release the emotions of frustration and despair. Rest in the plan of God and fully trust Him. You will discover that your disappointments can be transformed into great blessings in your life.

Get Growing!

- Based on today's passage, how can you change the way you handle disappointments in your life?
- Take a few minutes to bring your past disappointments to the Lord in prayer.

Salvation

But Zacchaeus stood up and said to the Lord, "Look, Lord! Here and now I give half my possessions to the poor, and if I have cheated anybody out of anything, I will pay back four times the amount." Jesus said to him. "Today salvation has come to this house, because this man, too, is a son of Abraham. For the Son of Man came to seek and to save the lost." Luke 19:8-10 (NIV)

The word "salvation" is used regularly in church, yet many people often fail to understand the full meaning of this word. What does it mean to be saved?

We find a story in the Gospel of Luke that provides us with a wonderful picture of both the process and results of salvation in a person's life. It's the story of a man named Zacchaeus. Jesus Christ had come to the city of Jericho. As usual, many people were eager to see him. They had heard the stories of his miracles. In the crowd that day, there was a man who was very lost and alone. Because he was a tax collector, he was not popular among the citizens of the city and was despised by many. The very nature of his position provided him the opportunity to take advantage of people. He had become wealthy at the expense of others. Yet Zacchaeus had an interest in seeing Christ. Being a short man, and because the crowds were so large, he climbed up into a tree to see Jesus as he passed through the city that day. But when Jesus came to that tree, he stopped and called out Zacchaeus' name. Zacchaeus came down from the tree and Jesus went to his house.

How did Christ know that Zacchaeus had experienced salvation? He knew it because of the radical change that occurred in his life. Zacchaeus was repentant of his lifestyle. When he was confronted with the love and grace of Jesus Christ, he was changed.

What does this word salvation mean? It is a word that is rich in meaning, but one thing it implies is a significant change of life.

Christ makes his salvation available to all who will call upon him. His salvation produces genuine, positive, and lifelong change in our lives.

Get Growing!

- Have you experienced the salvation that only comes through Jesus Christ? If not, I encourage you to call out to Christ today as Zacchaeus did and receive the salvation he offers.
- Have you ever witnessed somebody being saved by Jesus Christ? Were you able to see real change in the person's life?

Spiritual Paralysis

*Some men came, bringing to him a paralyzed man, carried
by four of them. Since they could not get him to Jesus
because of the crowd, they made an opening in the roof
above Jesus by digging through it and then lowered the
mat the man was lying on. When Jesus saw their faith, he
said to the paralyzed man, "Son, your sins are forgiven."*
Mark 2:3-5 (NIV)

In this passage, a large crowd had formed at a house
where Jesus was staying. As he preached to them, four
men brought a paralyzed man to be healed. Since the men
couldn't get through the crowd, they cut through the roof!
Can you imagine it? As Jesus was teaching, dust and dirt
began to fall. Then the sun appeared through a hole and
down came a paralyzed man on a mat!

When the paralyzed man came face to face with Jesus,
Jesus looked at the man and said, *"Son, your sins are
forgiven!"* From these words, we might assume that this
man's physical condition was the result of some kind of
sinful behavior. Whether or not that was true, it becomes
apparent that this man *thought* it was true. The most
desperate pain of this man was not physical, but spiritual.
He suffered not only from *physical paralysis*, but also from
spiritual paralysis.

Look what Jesus did for him. First, Jesus called this man
"son," which was a tender term like *"child."* In one word,
Jesus communicated acceptance, love, and trust. Then,
Jesus addressed the paralysis of the man's soul, *"your sins
are forgiven."* Jesus literally said, "all of your failures, all of
the mistakes of your life, all of the things that cause you to

feel unworthy and worthless, I am sending away from you by my forgiveness!" The man suddenly was free through the healing power of forgiveness. He was released from the paralysis of the soul and the paralysis of the body as well.

Many Christian believers today face something similar, a spiritual paralysis. Spiritual paralysis is the loss of spiritual motivation, zeal, and action. One of the most common causes is a deep-down struggle with failure and guilt that makes us feel unworthy and worthless.

Perhaps you feel this way today, or perhaps you know someone who does. Just as these four men brought the paralytic to Christ, we must come to Christ and hear his words of acceptance and love. We must fully receive his promise of grace and forgiveness, which brings healing to the paralysis of our soul.

Get Growing!

- Can you think of things that may be causing "spiritual paralysis" in your life? Bring them to the Lord and experience freedom.
- Sin paralyzes some people who can't or won't come to the Lord. They need good friends who will bring them to Jesus. How can you be that kind of friend?

Supernatural!

Jesus Christ is the same yesterday and today and forever.
Hebrews 13:8 (NIV)

For Jesus doesn't change—yesterday, today, tomorrow, he's
always totally himself. Hebrews 13:8 (MSG)

Do you believe in miracles? If your answer is yes, then you are a part of the majority. In a recent survey, eight out of ten people said they believe in miracles. Even folks who described themselves as non-religious affirmed a belief in the miraculous.

A miracle is defined as "a wonder, a marvel, an extraordinary event revealing or ascribed to divine intervention in human affairs." When God shows up in someone's life and does something good and beneficial that can't be explained by natural reasoning or natural laws, we know that the miraculous has happened.

The Bible is a supernatural book that, from the first chapter to the last, presents God as a living, caring, personal, miracle-working God. It shows us a God who actively intervenes in our world, and in people's lives with his power. He does things in and for people that cannot be explained by natural reasoning or natural laws.

Nowhere is this seen more clearly than in the life and ministry of Jesus Christ, the Son of God. Throughout his earthly ministry, he gave sight to the blind, hearing to the deaf, movement to the paralyzed, forgiveness to the shame-filled, and freedom and deliverance to people tortured and tormented by demon spirits. The greatest miracle of all was his resurrection from the dead!

This same Jesus does miracles today. Because Jesus is the same yesterday, today, and forever, we can approach him with confidence. Any time we face a need that is bigger than our capacity, a problem that defies our solutions, an impossibility that has limited or log-jammed our lives in some way, we can boldly run to him with hope and faith in his love for us, and in his power to help us.

Speaking of Jesus' love and care for us, and his willingness to miraculously help us, the writer of Hebrews described the right perspective in going to him with our needs: *"Let us then approach the throne of grace with confidence, so that we may receive mercy and find grace to help us in our time of need"* (Hebrews 4:16 NIV).

Whatever you are facing today, remember that the God of the Bible is a God who still does miracles. Through Jesus Christ, you can confidently approach him with your needs and trust him to do the supernatural in your life.

Get Growing!

Plan to read the Book of John in your daily devotional. As you do, ask the Holy Spirit to show you in a fresh way who the Jesus of *"yesterday, today and forever"* is. It will deepen and strengthen your faith!

Be Generous

Give, and it will be given to you. A good measure, pressed down, shaken together and running over, will be poured into your lap. For with the measure you use, it will be measured to you. Luke 6:38 (NIV)

... Remembering the words the Lord Jesus himself said: "It is more blessed to give than to receive." Acts 20:35 (NIV)

This quote from Jesus is a great life principle: "It is more blessed to give than to receive." This principle has been researched and proven to be true. People who give regularly are happier, healthier, and less stressed. Givers learn the joy of being a channel of blessings rather than a consumer of blessings. They enjoy passing on resources that help and encourage others. Their pleasure is found in "giving" more than in "getting."

Generous giving is one of the keys to a refreshed life. Inflow without outflow invites stagnation and disease. Look at a pond that gathers water without releasing it. All kinds of ugly things breed there. When people stop giving to God and others, their lives become stale and their hearts shrink. Ugly consequences show up in the souls of people who are stingy, selfish, and miserly.

The sad truth is, we live in a world of withholders. Emotional withholders damage marriages and friendships. Churches, ministries, and missions often struggle in fulfilling their calling because too few folks contribute time, talents, and treasures to the work. Productivity and advancements in organizations and businesses are restricted because people do not give their best efforts. Parsimony and stinginess of spirit never leads to anything good.

Here are six great reasons why generosity leads to great places:

- Generosity helps us be like God. God is generous. When you are generous, you are imitating him.
- Generosity frees us from stress and tension. Holding tight to anything brings fatigue. Release brings rest.
- Generosity attracts blessings. Generous means "magnanimous." The root word for magnanimous is "magnet." When we give, we attract blessings.
- Generosity demonstrates maturity. Small people live to get. Big (mature) people live to give.
- Generosity increases opportunities and influence. Greater opportunities come to people who invest their resources in others. When your heart is generously invested in something, your influence grows.
- Generosity reveals true faith and trust. When we give we are saying, "God, I trust you to take care of me!"

If you want the best life possible, make a decision to be a generous giver. Determine that absolutely nothing is going to stop you from giving. At the core of your being, believe the words of Jesus, "It's more blessed to give than to receive!"

Get Growing!

- What can you do to become a generous giver?
- When was the last time you gave generously? How did you feel?

Get Up and Get Going

Then Peter remembered the word Jesus had spoken: "Before the rooster crows, you will disown me three times." And he went outside and wept bitterly.
Matthew 26:75 (NIV)

Have you ever failed at something? Of course, we all have. No one learns to walk without stumbling and falling. It's likely that your first attempts at most new things failed. Failure is a part of learning, growing, of developing abilities and skills.

While it's easy and acceptable to embrace failure when it comes to new learning experiences, we sometimes struggle to get past other forms of failure—failed judgment, failed relationships, failed assignments, failed business. These often leave people with crippling shame and haunting regrets.

There's no doubt that some failures are more costly and serious than others. It's also true that certain kinds of failure should be avoided. We should never adopt a cavalier attitude about moral and character failures. We should never take lightly the impact of choosing sinful and evil actions over godly and good ones. These mistakes hurt God, us, and others. They often carry significant consequences.

So how does a person handle serious and significant failure? What should our response be to the mistakes and messes we make? How does a person deal with the consequences of mess-ups without becoming emotionally defeated and spiritually destroyed by them?

We get up and get going again! The consequences of certain failures have to be understood and appreciated, and messes have to be handled, but staying down does no one any good. Rising up, receiving God's forgiveness, seeking forgiveness from others, and forgiving ourselves is the way to turn things around.

The only one who wins when someone stays down is the devil. He loves to pound people with the ugly parts of their past. He's a master craftsman when it comes to condemnation. He sells you a lie that it's all over. He tries to make your failure final.

Many people in the Bible failed. The great Apostle Peter failed miserably. Yes, the guy that walked on water messed up. When Jesus needed him the most, Peter denied him, not once, but three times.

After Jesus rose from the dead, he went to Galilee and found Peter—despondent, defeated. Jesus restored Peter and got him going again. Not too many days later, after being filled with the Holy Spirit, this same man—Peter—preached the first recorded sermon of the church and three thousand people gave their lives to Jesus Christ. (Read Matthew 26:69-75; John 21:1-17; Acts 2:14-41.) That's a major turnaround! Jesus helped Peter get up and get going again.

If you've fallen, don't stay down. Get up and get going!

Get Growing!

- How do you handle your mistakes and failures? Do you tend to run to God for forgiveness or walk away in defeat?
- Why do you think God wants us to get up and get going?

How Compassionate Are You?

Be kind and compassionate to one another, forgiving each other, just as in Christ God forgave you.
Ephesians 4:32 (NIV)

Therefore, as God's chosen people, holy and dearly loved, clothe yourselves with compassion, kindness, humility, gentleness and patience. Colossians 3:12 (NIV)

All of us have read the accounts of individuals who were in extreme crisis situations and needed a compassionate hand from others, but were ignored. We have also read of the times of crisis where people have reached out a helping hand because of the compassion they felt in their hearts for those in need.

"Compassion" is an important word in the vocabulary of the Bible. As you study the nature of God both in the Old and New Testaments, you easily see a "God of compassion" shine through the pages. This characteristic is very evident in the life and ministry of our Lord.

In various passages of the New Testament we find that the Holy Spirit, through the pen of the writers, charges us as Christian believers with the responsibility of developing both a "heart of compassion" as well as "hands of compassion."

The passage above makes it clear that we are to be "people with compassionate hearts and hands." But how does this practically apply to us? What must we do and not do if we are to be people of compassion?

Let's look at three practical characteristics of godly compassion. First, godly compassion looks past faults to see and understand the needs of others. A truly compassionate person will not be constantly judging others actions and motives. Instead, they will attempt to understand the real needs present in the lives of others. Secondly, a compassionate heart makes one willing to sacrifice personal agendas and personal desires for the sake of others. Compassion moves a person beyond themselves and their own concerns to the concerns of others. Thirdly, the Jesus-kind of compassion moves a person to invest in helping others resolve the causes of their problems without a promise of anything in return. The compassion overcomes selfishness and self-centered pursuits.

Why is compassion such an important character trait to develop in our lives? Because compassionate people are the people who make a difference in the world. Without compassion, we become self-consumed and egocentric. Christ wants us to be people of compassion. He wants us to establish homes where compassion flows between husband and wife, parents and children. He desires for us to have churches that reflect his heart of compassion to a troubled world!

Get Growing!

- How about you today? Are you a compassionate person? Do you find it easy to invest yourself in helping others without judgment and resentment?
- Do you have the ability to let go of your own agendas; your time, energies, and resources for the sake of others?

Jesus Gives and Gives and...

*On the other side of the lake the crowds welcomed Jesus,
because they had been waiting for him. Then a man
named Jairus, a leader of the local synagogue, came and
fell at Jesus' feet, pleading with him to come home with
him. His only daughter, who was about twelve years old,
was dying. As Jesus went with him, he was surrounded
by the crowds. A woman in the crowd had suffered for
twelve years with constant bleeding, and she could find
no cure. Coming up behind Jesus, she touched the fringe
of his robe. Immediately, the bleeding stopped. "Who
touched me?" Jesus asked. Everyone denied it, and Peter
said, "Master, this whole crowd is pressing up against
you." But Jesus said, "Someone deliberately touched
me, for I felt healing power go out from me." When the
woman realized that she could not stay hidden, she began
to tremble and fell to her knees in front of him. The whole
crowd heard her explain why she had touched him and
that she had been immediately healed. "Daughter," he said
to her, "your faith has made you well. Go in peace."*
Luke 8:40-48 (NLT)

In this passage, we look at the story of Jesus' ministry
to the woman who had been bleeding for twelve years.
Although she had gone to many doctors and spent all she
had trying to get well, her efforts were all to no effect.

Desperation, humility, persistence, boldness, and faith
drove this woman to pursue Jesus and prompt the healing
to come from the Lord. When she touched Jesus' garment,
she was healed by the Lord. But Jesus went even farther
in his ministry to her. He *declared* her to be whole. Her

physical need was met, and Jesus also saved her soul and restored her emotionally.

This point brings to mind one of the great things about the Lord—his generous nature. When we approach God with our needs, he is not only inclined to meet our needs, he gives us more than what we ask for. This woman discovered the gracious and generous nature of Jesus that day. She learned that Jesus gives and gives and gives and....

The Apostle Paul later wrote that Jesus is able to do immeasurably more than all we ask or imagine, according to his power that is at work within us (Ephesians 3:20). This woman received more than she asked or imagined from Jesus that day. You will too. With faith, ask him for your needs and trust his love and generosity.

Get Growing!

- What would you like to humbly, persistently, boldly, and faithfully ask him to do for you?
- At this exact moment, you are in Jesus' presence. Take this opportunity to ask the Lord to help you.

Mouth Check

A truly wise person uses few words. Proverbs 17:27 (NLT)

Indeed, we all make many mistakes. For if we could control our tongues, we would be perfect and could also control ourselves in every other way. James 3:2 (NLT)

And the tongue is a flame of fire. It is full of wickedness, and poisons every part of the body. And the tongue is set on fire by hell itself and can turn our whole lives into a blazing flame of destruction and disaster. James 3:6 (TLB)

A couple of days ago as I was getting ready to head to the church office, I felt the gentle nudge of the Holy Spirit in my heart. It was one of those moments when I realized that he wanted to talk to me about something, or more specifically, to correct me about something.

In the quietness of this early morning encounter, the Lord reminded me of a statement I had made to someone the day before—a little comment that grieved the Lord. It really did not surprise me that he was bringing this to my attention. Although it was now about twelve hours past the event, I remembered feeling a twinge of conviction when I said it. However, because of the flow and fast-paced nature of the interaction at that moment, I had moved on without acknowledging or dealing with my comment immediately.

I had not said something profane, impure, irreverent or even unkind. I had not gossiped about someone. But I did make a quick comment that was insensitive and self-focused. And now, half a day later, God was bringing it back to my attention. It was something he was not willing to let slide.

As the Holy Spirit reminded me of my words, I felt the sting of Holy Spirit conviction in my heart. I felt sorrow as I saw myself and viewed my comment from God's perspective. In that moment, I asked the Lord for his forgiveness. I also asked him for the grace and power to be more careful with my words, and for the wisdom to deal with any hurt I may have caused. Let us learn to be eternally grateful for the Holy Spirit's persistence.

Get Growing!

- When was the last time God showed up in your life and talked to you about your words?
- What can you do to increase the control over your tongue?

Say No!

But Joseph refused. Genesis 39:8 (NLT)

"No" is a good word. If used it at the right times it can protect you from lots of pain and problems.

We are reminded of the value of a well-timed "no" when we read the Old Testament story of a young man named Joseph. After being betrayed by a group of jealous brothers and sold into slavery, Joseph found himself in Egypt. By providence, Joseph ended up serving a highly placed official in the Egyptian military named Potiphar. Joseph managed Potiphar's assets and activities so effectively that he was put in charge of all this man possessed.

Things were going great for Joseph until Potiphar's wife tried to seduce him. Joseph faced an intense moral test. He could say "yes" to Mrs. Potiphar and do what his flesh wanted to do, or he could say "no" to his urges and do what was right, knowing that this woman would likely hate him for it. What did Joseph do? *"Joseph refused..."*

The Hebrew word for "refused" used here is a strong one. It literally means "to reject; to disobey."

In the moment of temptation, Joseph's character shined with a strong, firm "NO!" This well-timed "no" was one of the pivotal points in Joseph's life. Had he said "yes" instead of "no," his story would probably not be in the Bible, or it certainly would be a very different one. Joseph's future—his destiny—was in large part set by his decision to say "no" at the right time—in the moment of his moral testing and temptation.

Go ahead. Say "no" to the things you need to say "no" to. Your destiny depends on it!

Get Growing!

- What do you need to say "no" to in your life?
- What test or temptation is demanding a "yes" from you while wisdom whispers a "no" in your soul?

Soft Hearts

... Plow up the hard ground of your hearts, for now is the time to seek the LORD, that he may come and shower righteousness upon you. Hosea 10:12 (NLT)

How soft is your heart? According to the dictionary, *"soft"* can be defined as "easy to mold; not hard or firm to the touch; having a pleasing quality; sympathetic or compassionate."

One of God's goals for each of us is to tenderize our hearts. Paul wrote to us: *Is there any encouragement from belonging to Christ? Any comfort from his love? Any fellowship together in the Spirit? Are your hearts tender and sympathetic?* (Philippians 2:1 NLT).

What does it mean to have a soft, tender heart? Several qualities mark a soft heart.

A soft heart is one that recognizes and receives God's voice when he speaks to us through his Word and by his Spirit about issues in our lives. God deals with us in a number of ways. He convicts us of sin. He reminds us of our commitments. He challenges us to change. He encourages us to keep pressing forward. Like a hard surface repelling water, hard hearts repel God's voice. A soft, tender heart recognizes and receives God's Word when it comes to call us to new levels of living.

A soft heart also responds promptly and obediently to God's dealings. When our hearts are tender, we quickly respond to God's correction by repenting of our sins and shortcomings. We don't delay our decision to be and do what God has convicted us to be and do. Tenderhearted people are responsive to God and to his workings in their lives.

How does a person develop a soft heart?

One of the ways we can tenderize our hearts is through extended seasons of prayer and fasting. As we set aside special times for seeking God, we invite him to rain his Spirit down upon the dry, hard areas of heart.

I encourage you to make fasting a part of your life. It's very important for your spiritual journey. Fasting is a great time to let God soften our hearts so that we recognize his voice, receive his Word and respond in prompt obedience to him.

Get Growing!

- How can you obtain and maintain a tender heart that is responsive to God and his work in your life?
- Take a few moments now to think about some ways you can include fasting in your life on a regular basis.

Yes, God Can!

David and all the Israelites marched to Jerusalem ...The Jebusites who lived there said to David, "You will not get in here." Nevertheless, David captured the fortress of Zion, the city of David. 1 Chronicles 11:4-5 (NIV)

Can or cannot? Possible or impossible? Opportunities or problems? These phrases represent the daily choices we make, how we choose to think and live, how we choose to respond to life circumstances and events. Will we approach life from a positive or negative perspective?

Many folks live a very restricted and limited life because of a negative mindset. Negative thinking results in negative reactions to the situations and challenges we experience. Negative reactions create more negative situations. Negativism causes us to perpetuate problems and pain. Wonderful things happen when we decisively and doggedly develop a spirit of faith.

David was a man who lived with a positive spirit of faith. When David decided to capture Jerusalem, and make it Israel's capital city, the people who lived there sent word to David that his plan would not work. They tried to convince David that taking their city would never happen. It could not be done. David would fail if he tried.

True to form, David ignored the negative words of doom and impossibility. I love the words the Bible uses to describe David's response to these folks, "Nevertheless, David captured the fortress..."

David was a man of faith. He was a man with a positive spirit. David was not moved by external obstacles or naysayers. David believed that God's plan was possible, and he acted on his beliefs. His faith inspired others to follow. Not only did David's belief bring him great rewards, it lifted other people to higher levels of life and accomplishment for the glory of God. It also attracted God's help and favor. David believed that God was leading him, and that God could and would help him. And, God did.

Whatever we are facing, let's remember, "Yes, God can!" And because God can, we can.

Get Growing!

- Are you easily affected by the negativity in your surroundings?
- How does negative thinking influence your life and your decisions?
- What is God saying to you today about your thoughts and attitude?

DALE A. O'SHIELDS

is the founding and senior pastor of Church of the Redeemer, a multi-cultural, multi-generational church with five campuses in the greater Washington, DC, area.

Pastor Dale is passionate about inspiring people to grow in Christ and impact their church and community. His practical teaching makes the Bible understandable and applicable in everyday life. His messages are broadcast widely and he has written several books and devotional resources. Pastor Dale invests in the next generation of church leaders through college-level classes and internship programs that prepare students for ministry through the local church.

In over thirty years of ministry, Pastor Dale has trained and equipped pastors, nationally and internationally, to plant and develop strong and thriving ministries. He founded the United Pastors Network to regularly invest in church leaders and teams.

Pastor Dale has been involved in pastoral ministry since 1978. He and his wife Terry have two married daughters and six grandchildren.

www.DaleOShields.com